THIRD EDITION

INTRO

Q

Skills for Success

LISTENING AND SPEAKING

Kevin McClure | Mari Vargo

D1294536

OXFORD
UNIVERSITY PRESS

OXFORD
UNIVERSITY PRESS

198 Madison Avenue
New York, NY 10016 USA

Great Clarendon Street, Oxford, OX2 6DP, United Kingdom

Oxford University Press is a department of the University of Oxford.
It furthers the University's objective of excellence in research, scholarship,
and education by publishing worldwide. Oxford is a registered trade
mark of Oxford University Press in the UK and in certain other countries

ISBN: 978 0 19 490512 1   STUDENT BOOK INTRO WITH IQ ONLINE PACK
ISBN: 978 0 19 490500 8   STUDENT BOOK INTRO AS PACK COMPONENT
ISBN: 978 0 19 490536 7   IQ ONLINE STUDENT WEBSITE

Printed in China

This book is printed on paper from certified and well-managed sources

ACKNOWLEDGEMENTS

Back cover photograph: Oxford University Press building/David Fisher

Illustrations by: emc design p. 80; 5W Infographics p. 93, p. 96.

*The Publishers would like to thank the following for their kind permission to
reproduce photographs and other copyright material:*

123rf: pp. 5 (hiker in mountains/maridav), 42 (berries/PaylessImages),
43 (meat/niloo138), (vegetables/foodandmore), (fruit/Giuseppe Elio
Cammarata), 44 (donuts/belchonock), 48 (milk/serezniy), 50 (market stall/
satina), 51 (salad/zazastudio), 53 (chilies/Natalia Klenova), 116 (fast food/
dolgachov), 133 (kayakers/langstrup); **Alamy:** pp. 10 (looking out of car
window/CSI Productions), 22 (student recreation room/Raul J Garcia), 30
(dorm room/Glasshouse Images), 33 (university library/PvE), 34 (fencing/
Stephen Shepherd), 43 (desserts/Pavel Kibenko), 48 (ingredients list/
FoodIngredients), 51 (eggs on toast/David Lee), 60 (shopping mall/__David
Gee), 63 (man reading book/Tetra Images), 64 (woman with umbrella/
Cultura Creative), (crowded city street/Alvey & Towers Picture Library), 72
(woman in scarf/Mint Images Limited), 75 (rollercoaster/Blaine Harrington
III), 85 (modern apartments/andrew parker), 86 (apartments to rent/
incamerastock), 88 (aerial view of settlement/mauritius images GmbH),
91 (swimming pool/Andreas von Einsiedel), (fireplace/Image Source
Plus), 102 (laughing bike shop assistant/Rimagine Group Limited), 112
(soccer player training/Tony Tallec), 113 (two students studying/Antonio
Guillem Fernández), 119 (two mountain bikers/Cultura Creative), 123
(rice terraces/Elena Ermakova), 125 (people crossing in Manhattan/
Littleny), (temple in Ubud/Peter Schickert), (canal in Bruges/kavalenkava
volha), 129 (young female traveler/Mariusz Szczawinski), 132 (fruit stall
in Dhaka/Maciej Dakowicz), 135 (architect/Tetra Images, LLC), 138 (Grand
Bazaar in Istanbul/Izel Photography), 139 (hand holding shells/Leszek
Czerwonka), 140 (Acropolis in Athens/nick baylis), 141 (Trafalgar square/
JOHN KELLERMAN), (British museum/Loop Images Ltd), (Globe theatre/
Ian Dagnall), 148 (girl in phone shop/Juice Images), 157 (Muslim bride
and groom/özkan özmen), 159 (boy on phone/Vadym Drobot), 161 (laptop/
Oleksiy Maksymenko Photography), 162 (train station ticket office/
Holmes Garden Photos); **Getty:** pp. cover (purple sequins on fabric/
Philippe Intraligi/EyeEm), 2 (painting mural/Cavan Images), 4 (young
group hiking forest/Hero Images), 5 (man playing soccer/Pornsawan
Sangmanee/EyeEm), (choir/Maskot), (woman cooking/mapodile), (men
playing game/10'000 Hours), 6 (baking cookies/ielanum), 9 (teacher
and children on fieldtrip/Hero Images), 11 (businessman on bike/Cavan
Images), 13 (painter/portishead1), 14 (scrabble/Science & Society Picture
Library), 17 (surfer/David Pu'u), 21 (young people collecting litter/
South_agency), 26 (woman waving at laptop/FatCamera), 31 (students
walking to school/Matt Henry Gunther), 37 (students in food hall/Frédéric
Soltan), 39 (college campus/HaizhanZheng), 40 (boats laden with food/
Wahyu Noviansyah/EyeEm), 45 (woman eating strawberries/andresr), 47
(family preparing to eat/PeopleImages), 57 (woman laughing /subman),
58 (beekeeper tending bees/Ian Lishman), 61 (family playing board game/
vgajic), 65 (young women on hiking trip/Tomas Rodriguez), 66 (young
men doing judo/Jun Tsukuda/Aflo), 70 (men jogging on road/Kaewmanee
Saekang/EyeEm), 71 (two friends playing basketball/Christopher Malcolm),
72 (man pondering/kupicoo), 76 (small house/Mireya Acierto), 78 (beach
front apartments/Arterra), 97 (Lofoten Islands/Roberto Moiola/Sysaworld),
98 (running club at sunrise/SolStock), 100 (tired woman/elenaleonova),
103 (family having breakfast/eli_asenova), 106 (pills spilled from bottles/
anilakkus), 111 (yoga teacher/Dean Mitchell), 120 (Kuala Lumpur/seng
chye teo), 128 (Museo Soumaya/Matt Mawson), 130 (woman in gallery/JGI/
Tom Grill), 135 (public speaker/Hero Images), 143 (student at Taj Mahal/
swissmediavision), 144 (sports crowd/simonkr), 152 (businessman on
laptop/Westend61), 153 (frustrated businessman/Jose Luis Pelaez Inc), 154
(frustrated woman with phone/JGI/Jamie Grill), 159 (frustrated woman
with laptop/Maskot), 163 (family relaxing in house/Maskot); **OUP:** pp. 5
(male tennis player/Shutterstock/VGstockstudio), 24 (university campus
in fall/Shutterstock/Jorge Salcedo), 51 (fast food/Shutterstock/Studio
37), 66 (skier/Shutterstock/Samot), 67 (potter making pot/Shutterstock/
MarinaGrigorivna), 68 (chairs on beach/Shutterstock/Sarah Jane Taylor),
(kite/Shutterstock/stable), (motorcycle/123rf/Bogdan Ionescu), 141 (Tower
of London/Shutterstock/donsimon); **Shutterstock:** pp. 15 (washing
car/Nomad_Soul), 28 (man taking notes/fizkes), 43 (dairy products/
bitt24), (whole grains/Tamakhin Mykhailo), 79 (city apartment building/
Sean Pavone), 90 (car in driveway/Imagenet), 104 (working and eating/
fizkes), 107 (taking vitamin pills/goffkein.pro), 109 (healthy salad bowl/
AnikonaAnn), 114 (man working late/mavo), 124 (Roman forum ruins/
Nejron Photo), 147 (old cellphone/Ayah Raushan), 161 (smartphone/
OSABEE), (smartwatch/BallBall14); **Third party:** pp. 89 (Jack Sparrow
house/Jonathan Melville-Smith), 156 (Esplorio app logo/Esplorio).

We would like to acknowledge the teachers from all over the world who participated in the development process and review of Q: *Skills for Success* Third Edition.

USA

Kate Austin, Avila University, MO; **Sydney Bassett**, Auburn Global University, AL; **Michael Beamer**, USC, CA; **Renae Betten**, CBU, CA; **Pepper Boyer**, Auburn Global University, AL; **Marina Broeder**, Mission College, CA; **Thomas Brynmore**, Auburn Global University, AL; **Britta Burton**, Mission College, CA; **Kathleen Castello**, Mission College, CA; **Teresa Cheung**, North Shore Community College, MA; **Shantall Colebrooke**, Auburn Global University, AL; **Kyle Cooper**, Troy University, AL; **Elizabeth Cox**, Auburn Global University, AL; **Ashley Ekers**, Auburn Global University, AL; **Rhonda Farley**, Los Rios Community College, CA; **Marcus Frame**, Troy University, AL; **Lora Glaser**, Mission College, CA; **Hala Hamka**, Henry Ford College, MI; **Shelley A. Harrington**, Henry Ford College, MI; **Barrett J. Heusch**, Troy University, AL; **Beth Hill**, St. Charles Community College, MO; **Patty Jones**, Troy University, AL; **Tom Justice**, North Shore Community College, MA; **Robert Klein**, Troy University, AL; **Patrick Maestas**, Auburn Global University, AL; **Elizabeth Merchant**, Auburn Global University, AL; **Rosemary Miketa**, Henry Ford College, MI; **Myo Myint**, Mission College, CA; **Lance Noe**, Troy University, AL; **Irene Pannatier**, Auburn Global University, AL; **Annie Percy**, Troy University, AL; **Erin Robinson**, Troy University, AL; **Juliane Rosner**, Mission College, CA; **Mary Stevens**, North Shore Community College, MA; **Pamela Stewart**, Henry Ford College, MI; **Karen Tucker**, Georgia Tech, GA; **Loreley Wheeler**, North Shore Community College, MA; **Amanda Wilcox**, Auburn Global University, AL; **Heike Williams**, Auburn Global University, AL

Canada

Angelika Brunel, Collège Ahuntsic, QC; **David Butler**, English Language Institute, BC; **Paul Edwards**, Kwantlen Polytechnic University, BC; **Cody Hawver**, University of British Columbia, BC; **Olivera Jovovic**, Kwantlen Polytechnic University, BC; **Tami Moffatt**, University of British Columbia, BC; **Dana Pynn**, Vancouver Island University, BC

Latin America

Georgette Barreda, SENATI, Peru; **Claudia Cecilia Díaz Romero**, Colegio América, Mexico; **Jeferson Ferro**, Uninter, Brazil; **Mayda Hernández**, English Center, Mexico; **Jose Ixtaccihusatl**, Instituto Tecnológico de Tecomatlán, Mexico; **Andreas Paulus Pabst**, CBA Idiomas, Brazil; **Amanda Carla Pas**, Instituição de Ensino Santa Izildinha, Brazil; **Allen Quesada Pacheco**, University of Costa Rica, Costa Rica; **Rolando Sánchez**, Escuela Normal de Tecámac, Mexico; **Luis Vasquez**, CESNO, Mexico

Asia

Asami Atsuko, Jissen Women's University, Japan; **Rene Bouchard**, Chinzei Keiai Gakuen, Japan; **Francis Brannen**, Sangmyung University, South Korea; **Haeyun Cho**, Sogang University, South Korea; **Daniel Craig**, Sangmyung University, South Korea; **Thomas Cuming**, Royal Melbourne Institute of Technology, Vietnam; **Nguyen Duc Dat**, OISP, Vietnam; **Wayne Devitte**, Tokai University, Japan; **James D. Dunn**, Tokai University, Japan; **Fergus Hann**, Tokai University, Japan; **Michael Hood**, Nihon University College of Commerce, Japan; **Hideyuki Kashimoto**, Shijonawate High School, Japan; **David Kennedy**, Nihon University, Japan; **Anna Youngna Kim**, Sogang University, South Korea; **Jae Phil Kim**, Sogang University, South Korea; **Jaganathan Krishnasamy**, GB Academy, Malaysia; **Peter Laver**, Incheon National University, South Korea; **Hung Hoang Le**, Ho Chi Minh City University of Technology, Vietnam; **Hyon Sook Lee**, Sogang University, South Korea; **Ji-seon Lee**, Iruda English Institute, South Korea; **Joo Young Lee**, Sogang University, South Korea; **Phung Tu Luc**, Ho Chi Minh City University of Technology, Vietnam; **Richard Mansbridge**, Hoa Sen University, Vietnam; **Kahoko Matsumoto**, Tokai University, Japan; **Elizabeth May**, Sangmyung University, South Korea; **Naoyuki Naganuma**, Tokai University, Japan; **Hiroko Nishikage**, Taisho University, Japan; **Yongjun Park**, Sangji University, South Korea; **Paul Rogers**, Dongguk University, South Korea; **Scott Schafer**, Inha University, South Korea; **Michael Schvaudner**, Tokai University, Japan; **Brendan Smith**, RMIT University, School of Languages and English, Vietnam; **Peter Snashall**, Huachiew Chalermprakiet University, Thailand; **Makoto Takeda**, Sendai Third Senior High School, Japan; **Peter Talley**, Mahidol University, Faculty of ICT, Thailand; **Byron Thigpen**, Sogang University, South Korea; **Junko Yamaai**, Tokai University, Japan; **Junji Yamada**, Taisho University, Japan; **Sayoko Yamashita**, Jissen Women's University, Japan; **Masami Yukimori**, Taisho University, Japan

Middle East and North Africa

Sajjad Ahmad, Taibah University, Saudi Arabia; **Basma Alansari**, Taibah University, Saudi Arabia; **Marwa Al-ashqar**, Taibah University, Saudi Arabia; **Dr. Rashid Al-Khawaldeh**, Taibah University, Saudi Arabia; **Mohamed Almohamed**, Taibah University, Saudi Arabia; **Dr. Musaad Alrahaili**, Taibah University, Saudi Arabia; **Hala Al Sammar**, Kuwait University, Kuwait; **Ahmed Alshammari**, Taibah University, Saudi Arabia; **Ahmed Alshamy**, Taibah University, Saudi Arabia; **Doniazad sultan AlShraideh**, Taibah University, Saudi Arabia; **Sahar Amer**, Taibah University, Saudi Arabia; **Nabeela Azam**, Taibah University, Saudi Arabia; **Hassan Bashir**, Edex, Saudi Arabia; **Rachel Batchilder**, College of the North Atlantic, Qatar; **Nicole Cuddie**, Community College of Qatar, Qatar; **Mahdi Duris**, King Saud University, Saudi Arabia; **Ahmed Ege**, Institute of Public Administration, Saudi Arabia; **Magda Fadle**, Victoria College, Egypt; **Mohammed Hassan**, Taibah University, Saudi Arabia; **Tom Hodgson**, Community College of Qatar, Qatar; **Ayub Agbar Khan**, Taibah University, Saudi Arabia; **Cynthia Le Joncour**, Taibah University, Saudi Arabia; **Ruari Alexander MacLeod**, Community College of Qatar, Qatar; **Nasir Mahmood**, Taibah University, Saudi Arabia; **Duria Salih Mahmoud**, Taibah University, Saudi Arabia; **Ameera McKoy**, Taibah University, Saudi Arabia; **Chaker Mhamdi**, Buraimi University College, Oman; **Baraa Shiekh Mohamed**, Community College of Qatar, Qatar; **Abduleelah Mohammed**, Taibah University, Saudi Arabia; **Shumaila Nasir**, Taibah University, Saudi Arabia; **Kevin Onwordi**, Taibah University, Saudi Arabia; **Dr. Navid Rahmani**, Community College of Qatar, Qatar; **Dr. Sabah Salman Sabbah**, Community College of Qatar, Qatar; **Salih**, Taibah University, Saudi Arabia; **Verna Santos-Nafrada**, King Saud University, Saudi Arabia; **Gamal Abdelfattah Shehata**, Taibah University, Saudi Arabia; **Ron Stefan**, Institute of Public Administration, Saudi Arabia; **Dr. Saad Torki**, Imam Abdulrahman Bin Faisal University, Dammam, Saudi Arabia; **Silvia Yafai**, Applied Technology High School/Secondary Technical School, UAE; **Mahmood Zar**, Taibah University, Saudi Arabia; **Thouraya Zheni**, Taibah University, Saudi Arabia

Turkey

Sema Babacan, Istanbul Medipol University; **Bilge Çöllüoğlu Yakar**, Bilkent University; **Liana Corniel**, Koc University; **Savas Geylanioglu**, Izmir Bahcesehir Science and Technology College; **Öznur Güler**, Giresun University; **Selen Bilginer Halefoğlu**, Maltepe University; **Ahmet Konukoğlu**, Hasan Kalyoncu University; **Mehmet Salih Yoğun**, Gaziantep Hasan Kalyoncu University; **Fatih Yücel**, Beykent University

Europe

Amina Al Hashamia, University of Exeter, UK; **Irina Gerasimova**, Saint-Petersburg Mining University, Russia; **Jodi**, Las Dominicas, Spain; **Marina Khanykova**, School 179, Russia; **Oksana Postnikova**, Lingua Practica, Russia; **Nina Vasilchenko**, Soho-Bridge Language School, Russia

CRITICAL THINKING

The unique critical thinking approach of the *Q: Skills for Success* series has been further enhanced in the Third Edition. New features help you analyze, synthesize, and develop your ideas.

Unit question
The thought-provoking unit questions engage you with the topic and provide a critical thinking framework for the unit.

 UNIT QUESTION

How do you use technology?

A. Discuss these questions with your classmates.
1. Look at the photo. What kind of technology do you see?
2. How do you think these people are using the technology?
3. How do you use this type of technology?

Analysis
You can discuss your opinion of each listening text and analyze how it changes your perspective on the unit question.

 SAY WHAT YOU THINK

SYNTHESIZE Think about Listening 1, Listening 2, and the unit video as you discuss the questions.
1. How do you feel when you forget your cell phone? Why?
2. Do you think cell phones make life easier or harder? Explain.
3. Imagine that nobody has a cell phone. How is your life different? Think of five examples.

CRITICAL THINKING STRATEGY

Relating to ideas
To **relate** to an idea is to connect yourself to it. Relating to an idea helps you understand it better. When you learn about a new idea, think about your opinions about it or how it might affect you.

iQ PRACTICE Go online to watch the Critical Thinking Video and check your comprehension. *Practice › Unit 6 › Activity 9*

NEW! Critical Thinking Strategy with video
Each unit includes a Critical Thinking Strategy with activities to give you step-by-step guidance in critical analysis of texts. An accompanying instructional video (available on iQ Online) provides extra support and examples.

E. CATEGORIZE Read the meal descriptions in Activity D again. How are they similar to or different from your diet? Take notes in the chart. Then rank the diets from 1 (most similar to yours) to 4 (least similar to yours). Share with a partner.

Others' diets	Similarities to my diet	Differences from my diet	Ranking
1. Nour			
2. Alex			
3. Cynthia			
4. Pedro			

NEW! Bloom's Taxonomy
Blue activity headings integrate verbs from Bloom's Taxonomy to help you see how each activity develops critical thinking skills.

F. CREATE Write answers to the questions.
1. What do you usually eat for breakfast, lunch, and dinner?

_____

_____

_____

2. Do you think you have a balanced diet? Explain.

_____

_____

3. Based on your answers to questions 1 and 2, do you think you should take supplements? Why or why not?

_____

THREE TYPES OF VIDEO

UNIT VIDEO

The unit videos include high-interest documentaries and reports on a wide variety of subjects, all linked to the unit topic and question.

NEW! "Work with the Video" pages guide you in watching, understanding, and discussing the unit videos. The activities help you see the connection to the Unit Question and the other texts in the unit.

CRITICAL THINKING VIDEO

NEW! Narrated by the *Q* series authors, these short videos give you further instruction on the Critical Thinking Strategy of each unit using engaging images and graphics. You can use them to gain a deeper understanding of the Critical Thinking Strategy.

SKILLS VIDEO

NEW! These instructional videos provide illustrated explanations of skills and grammar points in the Student Book. They can be viewed in class or assigned for a flipped classroom, for homework, or for review. One skill video is available for every unit.

Easily access all videos in the Resources section of iQ Online.

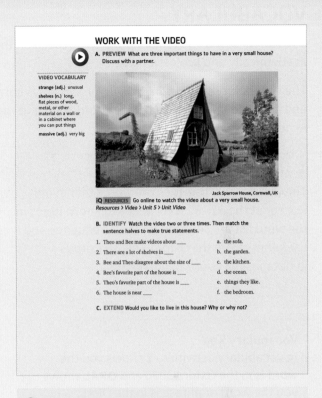

WORK WITH THE VIDEO

A. PREVIEW What are three important things to have in a very small house? Discuss with a partner.

VIDEO VOCABULARY

strange (adj.) unusual

shelves (n.) long, flat pieces of wood, metal, or other material on a wall or in a cabinet where you can put things

massive (adj.) very big

Jack Sparrow House, Cornwall, UK

iQ RESOURCES Go online to watch the video about a very small house.
Resources > Video > Unit 5 > Unit Video

B. IDENTIFY Watch the video two or three times. Then match the sentence halves to make true statements.

1. Theo and Bee make videos about ____
2. There are a lot of shelves in ____
3. Bee and Theo disagree about the size of ____
4. Bee's favorite part of the house is ____
5. Theo's favorite part of the house is ____
6. The house is near ____

a. the sofa.
b. the garden.
c. the kitchen.
d. the ocean.
e. things they like.
f. the bedroom.

C. EXTEND Would you like to live in this house? Why or why not?

How to compare and contrast

Venn Diagram

Firefighter — Both — Police Officer

fights fires — *help people* — *fights crime*

stays at the station until called — *have dangerous jobs* — *works on the street*

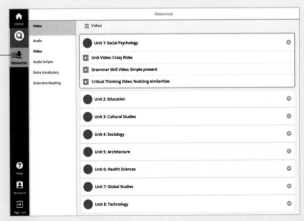

VOCABULARY

A research-based vocabulary program focuses on the words you need to know academically and professionally.

The vocabulary syllabus in *Q: Skills for Success* is correlated to the CEFR (see page 164) and linked to two word lists: the Oxford 3000 and the OPAL (Oxford Phrasal Academic Lexicon).

⚷ OXFORD 3000

The Oxford 3000 lists the core words that every learner at the A1–B2 level needs to know. Items in the word list are selected for their frequency and usefulness from the Oxford English Corpus (a database of over 2 billion words).

Vocabulary Key
In vocabulary activities, ⚷ shows you the word is in the Oxford 3000 and **OPAL** shows you the word or phrase is in the OPAL.

PREVIEW THE LISTENING

A. VOCABULARY Here are some words from Listening 2. Read the definitions. Then complete the sentences below.

affordable *(adjective)* not expensive
condition *(noun)* ⚷ OPAL something in good condition is not damaged or broken
demand *(noun)* ⚷ OPAL a need or want
entertainment *(noun)* ⚷ fun or free-time activities
housing *(noun)* ⚷ apartments, houses, and homes
increase *(verb)* ⚷ OPAL to become bigger
landlord *(noun)* a person—he or she rents homes to people for money
shortage *(noun)* not enough of something

⚷ Oxford 3000™ words   OPAL Oxford Phrasal Academic Lexicon

OPAL
OXFORD PHRASAL ACADEMIC LEXICON

NEW! The OPAL is a collection of four word lists that provide an essential guide to the most important words and phrases to know for academic English. The word lists are based on the Oxford Corpus of Academic English and the British Academic Spoken English corpus. The OPAL includes both spoken and written academic English and both individual words and longer phrases.

Academic Language tips in the Student Book give information about how words and phrases from the OPAL are used and offer help with features such as collocations and phrases.

ACADEMIC LANGUAGE
You can use *available* with or without the preposition *to* after it. You can use different verbs before *available*: *be available*, *become available*, *make* (something) *available*.

⌐──────────────⌐ OPAL
Oxford Phrasal Academic Lexicon

1. I couldn't go online with my old cell phone. It wa:
   a. You can go online with a smartphone.
   b. You can't go online with a smartphone.

2. The new cell phone is not <u>available</u> to buyers yet. next Monday.
   a. You can buy the new cell phone now.
   b. You can't buy the new cell phone now.

3. Eric is <u>working on</u> his paper. It's due on Wednesd
   a. Eric is at work.
   b. Eric is writing his paper.

4. I can send you <u>text messages</u> while I'm at work, b
   a. A text message is the same thing as a phone ca
   b. A text message is not the same thing as a phor

5. Margo <u>keeps in touch</u> with her old friends. She li! they're doing.
   a. When you keep in touch with someone, you se
   b. When you keep in touch with someone, you d

EXTENSIVE READING

NEW! Extensive Reading is a program of reading for pleasure at a level that matches your language ability.

There are many benefits to Extensive Reading:

- It helps you to become a better reader in general.
- It helps to increase your reading speed.
- It can improve your reading comprehension.
- It increases your vocabulary range.
- It can help you improve your grammar and writing skills.
- It's great for motivation to read something that is interesting for its own sake.

Each unit of *Q: Skills for Success* Third Edition has been aligned to an Oxford Graded Reader based on the appropriate topic and level of language proficiency. The first chapter of each recommended graded reader can be downloaded from iQ Online Resources.

UNIT 1

UNIT 2

UNIT 3

UNIT 4

UNIT 5

UNIT 6

UNIT 7

UNIT 8

iQ ONLINE extends your learning beyond the classroom.

- Practice activities provide essential skills practice and support.
- Automatic grading and progress reports show you what you have mastered and where you need more practice.
- The Discussion Board allows you to discuss the Unit Questions and helps you develop your critical thinking.
- Essential resources such as audio and video are easy to access anytime.

NEW TO THE THIRD EDITION

- iQ Online is optimized for mobile use so you can use it on your phone.
- An updated interface allows easy navigation around the activities, tests, resources, and scores.
- New Critical Thinking Videos expand on the Critical Thinking Strategies in the Student Book.
- The Extensive Reading program helps you improve your vocabulary and reading skills.

How to use iQ ONLINE

Go to **Practice** to find additional practice and support to complement your learning in the classroom.

Go to **Resources** to find:
- All Student Book video
- All Student Book audio
- Critical Thinking videos
- Skills videos
- Extensive Reading

Go to **Messages** and **Discussion Board** to communicate with your teacher and classmates.

Online tests assigned by your teacher help you assess your progress and see where you need more practice.

A progress bar shows you how many activities you have completed.

View your scores for all activities.

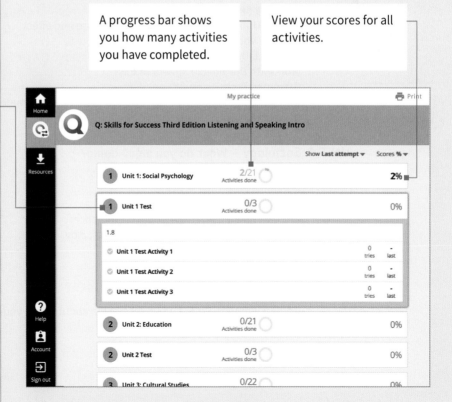

CONTENTS

Social Psychology

CRITICAL THINKING	noticing similarities
VOCABULARY	collocations for hobbies and interests
GRAMMAR	simple present of *be*; simple present of other verbs
PRONUNCIATION	simple present third-person *-s*/*-es*
SPEAKING	keeping a conversation going
NOTE-TAKING	writing important words

What are you interested in?

A. Discuss these questions with your classmates.

1. What do you talk about with a new friend? Circle the topics. Add one topic.

music	photos you see online
sports	family
movies	work
books	_____
videos you see online	

2. What activities do you like?

3. Look at the photo. What is this person doing? Are you interested in this activity?

B. Listen to *The Q Classroom* online. Then answer these questions.

1. What did the students say? What are they interested in?

2. Do the students like the same things you like?

iQ PRACTICE Go to the online discussion board to discuss the Unit Question with your classmates. *Practice > Unit 1 > Activity 1*

UNIT OBJECTIVE Listen to a radio program. Use information and ideas to interview a classmate. Then introduce him or her to the class.

LISTENING

OBJECTIVE ▶

Are You Interested in Hiking?

You are going to listen to a radio discussion at a school. Think about what interests you.

PREVIEW THE LISTENING

A. VOCABULARY Here are some words and phrases from the listening. Read the definitions. Then circle the correct word or phrase to complete each conversation.

ACADEMIC LANGUAGE

Interested is one of the most common academic words. *Interested in* is a common spoken phrase. Speakers often use the phrase at the beginning of a lesson to focus on a topic.

_____ **OPAL**
Oxford Phrasal Academic Lexicon

> **belong to** *(verb phrase)* 🔑 to be a member of a group
> **club** *(noun)* 🔑 a group of people—they meet and do things together
> **collect** *(verb)* 🔑 to get and keep many things because you like them
> **good at** *(phrase)* 🔑 can do something well
> **hobbies** *(noun)* 🔑 activities—you do them for fun
> **interested in** *(phrase)* 🔑 OPAL enjoying an activity or a topic
> **team** *(noun)* 🔑 a group of people—they play a sport or a game together

🔑 Oxford 3000 keywords   **OPAL** Oxford Phrasal Academic Lexicon

1. A: Do you (collect / (belong to)) the math club?

   B: Yes, I do. We meet on Thursdays.

2. A: I like basketball, but I can't play it well.

   B: My roommate is very (good at / team) basketball. He can teach you.

3. A: Wow, you're a great soccer player! Are you on the soccer (hobbies / team)?

   B: Thanks! Yes, I am.

4. A: What do you like to do?

   B: Oh, I have a lot of (interested in / hobbies). I play tennis, I go hiking, and I like poetry.

5. A: Is there a book (team / club) at this school?

   B: Yes, there is. We meet in the library every Wednesday night. It's fun!

6. A: You have a lot of postcards!

   B: I (hobbies / collect) them. I have more than 2,000 postcards.

7. A: I like the museum. Are you (belong to / interested in) history?

   B: Yes. History is my favorite class.

iQ PRACTICE Go online for more practice with the vocabulary.
Practice > Unit 1 > Activities 2–3

B. CATEGORIZE Read the sentences. Write *T* (true) or *F* (false). Then correct the false statements. Compare your answers with a partner.

____ 1. I collect coins. _____

____ 2. I belong to a book club. _____

____ 3. I am interested in sports. _____

____ 4. I am good at writing. _____

____ 5. My hobbies are soccer and cooking. _____

C. PREVIEW You are going to listen to a radio discussion. The speakers talk about hobbies, or things they like to do. Look at the photos. Match the hobby with the photo.

____ cooking   ____ hiking   ____ singing

____ soccer   ____ tennis   ____ video games

WORK WITH THE LISTENING

🔊 **A. CATEGORIZE** Read the sentences. Then listen to the discussion. Write *T* (true), *F* (false), or *N* (not enough information).

iQ RESOURCES Go online to download extra vocabulary support.
Resources > *Extra Vocabulary* > *Unit 1*

_____ 1. All the speakers are students.

_____ 2. All the speakers have hobbies.

_____ 3. All the speakers play sports.

_____ 4. Some of the speakers belong to clubs.

_____ 5. Some of the speakers are new students.

🔊 **B. IDENTIFY** Listen again. What are the people interested in? Check (✓) the correct activities.

	Sara	Hiro	Daniel	Ben	Mei
clubs	☐	☐	☐	☐	☐
teams	☐	☐	☐	☐	☐
hiking	☐	☐	☐	☐	☐
music	☐	☐	☐	☐	☐
soccer	☐	☐	☐	☐	☐
photography	☐	☐	☐	☐	☐
tennis	☐	☐	☐	☐	☐
math	☐	☐	☐	☐	☐
video games	☐	☐	☐	☐	☐
baking/cooking	☐	☐	☐	☐	☐
getting together with friends on weekends	☐	☐	☐	☐	☐

baking cookies

 CRITICAL THINKING STRATEGY

Noticing similarities

When you hear information about different things or people, some information may be the same or similar.

- Listen for words that show things that are the same.

- You can also listen for words that are different but have the same, or a similar, meaning. These words are called **synonyms**.

Noticing similarities can help you group or categorize the information you hear.

Information	Similarities
Anita in interested in music and <u>art</u>. Hugo is interested in <u>art</u> and sports.	Both Anita and Hugo are interested in art.
Cara enjoys <u>hiking</u>. Steven likes <u>walking outdoors</u> and <u>climbing mountains</u>.	Both Cara and Steven enjoy hiking. (Hiking is a type of walking outdoors. These words are synonyms.)
Michael plays <u>tennis</u> and <u>baseball</u>. Lucy plays <u>basketball</u>. Xander is on the <u>soccer</u> team.	Michael, Lucy, and Xander all play sports: tennis, baseball, basketball, and soccer.

iQ PRACTICE Go online to watch the Critical Thinking Video and check your comprehension. *Practice > Unit 1 > Activity 4*

C. **INVESTIGATE** Interview three or more of your classmates about how they feel today. Take notes. Try to notice similarities in their responses and report back to the class.

D. **ANALYZE** Look at the chart in Activity B. Complete the sentences about similarities. Then compare your answers with a partner.

1. _____, _____, and _____ belong to clubs.

2. _____ and _____ are on a soccer team.

3. _____ and _____ are interested in photography.

4. _____ and _____ like to bake or cook.

5. _____, _____, _____, and _____ get together with friends on weekends.

E. **CREATE** Look at the chart in Activity B again. Answer the questions.

1. Which person is the most similar to you? _____

2. How are you and that person similar? What things do you do that are the same?

   _____

3. Are you similar to any of the other speakers? If so, who else are you similar to and how? _____

   _____

🔊 **F. IDENTIFY** Listen again. Circle the correct answer.

1. Mei's last name is ____.

   a. Lee   b. Cheng   c. Thien

2. Sara ____ with a group.

   a. sings   b. plays music   c. runs

3. Hiro reads ____.

   a. the newspaper   b. books on history   c. video game
   every day   magazines

4. Daniel is good at ____.

   a. history   b. music   c. math

5. Ben likes to collect ____.

   a. baseball hats   b. postcards   c. pens

iQ PRACTICE Go online for additional listening and comprehension.
Practice > Unit 1 > Activity 5

BUILDING VOCABULARY Collocations for hobbies and interests

Some words usually go together. These are called **collocations**.

Verb (phrase) + preposition + noun	Verb + noun
be good at volleyball / math	**go** shopping / hiking
be interested in books / sports	**play** sports / tennis / games
be on a team	**read** books / magazines
belong to a book club	**ride** a bicycle / a bike
get together with friends	**take** lessons
go to a museum / the beach / a park	**watch** a movie / television (TV)
listen to the radio	
live in Tokyo	

🔊 **A. APPLY** Complete the collocations with words from the box above.
Then listen to check your answers.

Alan lives _____ 1 Toronto. He works at the after-school program

at the community center in his town. Children come to the community

center after school. Alan does many activities with them. It's a good job for

him because he is interested _____ 2 a lot of different things.

He is good _____ 3 sports. On sunny days, Alan and the kids

_____ bikes or _____ hiking. Sometimes they
    4   5

go _____ the beach or the park. On rainy days, Alan and the
      6

kids _____ movies, or they _____ games like
        7   8

Scrabble and checkers. Sometimes they _____ to a museum
                                               9

together. After work, Alan sometimes gets _____ with friends,
                                                  10

but he usually goes home to relax and _____ a book.
                                              11

B. RESTATE Listen to the people talk about themselves. Write two sentences about each speaker. Use the words in parentheses.

1. **Saud** (reads) _____

   (is interested in) _____

2. **Khalid** (plays) _____

   (rides) _____

C. CREATE Write three sentences about you. Use collocations from the box on page 8.

1. _____

2. _____

3. _____

iQ PRACTICE   Go online for more practice with collocations for hobbies and interests. *Practice ▸ Unit 1 ▸ Activity 6*

WORK WITH THE VIDEO

A. PREVIEW How do you get around your town or city? What kinds of transportation do you take?

iQ **RESOURCES** Go online to watch the video about someone's hobby.
Resources > Video > Unit 1 > Unit Video

B. ANALYZE Watch the video two or three times. Take notes in the first part of the chart.

	Questions about hobbies	Answers
Notes from the video	What does Mark love?	
	What did he make into a car?	
	What changes did he make?	
	How long did it take?	
	How much did it cost?	
	What does he do with his car?	
My hobby	What is it?	
	How much does it cost?	
	How much time do you spend on it?	

C. EXTEND Think about one of your hobbies. Write your ideas in the chart above.

SAY WHAT YOU THINK

A. INVESTIGATE Go around the class. Ask the questions from the chart. When someone answers *yes*, write down his or her name. Try to write a different name for each question.

I ride a bicycle to class.

A: Do you ride a bicycle to class?
B: Yes, I do.

Question	Name
1. Do you belong to a club?	
2. Are you interested in books?	
3. Do you play tennis?	
4. Are you good at math?	
5. Are you on a sports team?	
6. Do you ride a bicycle to class?	
7. Do you get together with friends on Thursdays?	
8. Do you take any lessons?	

B. DISCUSS Share your answers with a group.

A: Eric belongs to a soccer club.
B: Alex belongs to a soccer club, too.

TIP FOR SUCCESS
Use the word *too* to add information. It has the same meaning as *also*.

SPEAKING

OBJECTIVE ▶   At the end of this unit, you are going to interview a classmate and introduce him or her to the class.

GRAMMAR   *Part 1* Simple present of *be*

Use the verb *be* to identify and describe people and things.

TIP FOR SUCCESS

Statements with *be* are followed by nouns (*student*), adjectives (*tired*), or prepositional phrases (*from China*).

Statements

subject	*be*	(*not*)	
I	**am / 'm**		a student.
You / We / They	**are / 're**	**(not)**	tired.
He / She / It	**is / 's**		from China.

- A contraction makes two words into one word. It has an apostrophe (').

  I am = I'm   You are = You're   They are = They're
  He is = He's   She is = She's   It is = It's

- You usually use contractions in speaking.

- There are two negative contractions for *are not*.

  are not = 're not / aren't
  They**'re not** happy.   They **aren't** tired.

- There are two negative contractions for *is not*.

  is not = 's not / isn't
  She**'s not** American.   He **isn't** from England.

	Yes / No questions		Answers
be	subject		
Are	you / we / they	in class?	Yes, I **am**. / No, we**'re not**. / Yes, they **are**.
Is	he / she		No, she **isn't**. / Yes, he **is**.

	Information questions			Answers
wh- word	*be*	subject		
What	**is**	she	interested in?	She**'s** interested in sports.
Where	**are**	they	from?	They**'re** from Morocco.
How old	**are**	you?		I**'m** 22 years old.

- You can give short answers or long answers:

  A: How old are you?
  B: 18. / I'm 18 years old.

A. APPLY Complete the sentences with the correct form of *be*.

1. Mauro _is_ an artist. He _isn't_ (not) from Colombia. He _____ from Peru.

2. Rika and Emiko _____ students. Rika _____ in my English class. Emiko _____ in my chemistry class. They _____ from Japan.

3. Feride _____ (not) American. She _____ Turkish.

4. I _____ (not) from England. I _____ from Ireland.

5. We _____ (not) interested in sports. We _____ interested in movies.

B. COMPOSE Put the words in the correct order. Then ask and answer the questions with a partner.

1. you / from / where / are _Where are you from?_____

2. interested / hiking / you / in / are _____

3. at / you / are / what / good _____

4. years / 20 / old / you / are _____

GRAMMAR *Part 2* Simple present of other verbs

Use the simple present with other verbs to describe habits, facts, and feelings.

Affirmative statements		
subject	verb	
I / You / We / They	**play**	soccer.
He / She	**plays**	tennis.

Negative statements			
subject	*do / does + not*	verb	
I / You / We / They	**do not / don't**	**play**	baseball.
He / She	**does not / doesn't**		

- Use *do not* with *I, we, you,* and *they.*
- Use *does not* with *he, she,* and *it.*

Yes / No questions				Answers
do / does	subject	verb		
Do	you / we / they	**like**	tennis?	Yes, I **do.** / No, we **don't.** / Yes, they **do.**
Does	he / she			Yes, he **does.** / No, she **doesn't.**

Information questions				Answers
wh- word	*do / does*	subject		
What	**do**	you	play?	I play soccer.
Where	**does**	he	live?	He lives in Seoul.
When	**do**	they	study?	At 6:00.

- You can give short answers or long answers for these questions, too:

    A: Where do you live?

    B: In Tokyo. / I live in Tokyo.

iQ RESOURCES Go online to watch the Grammar Skill Video.
Resources > Video > Unit 1 > Grammar Skill Video

C. APPLY Complete the conversations with the verbs from the box. Use the correct form. You will use some verbs more than once. Then practice with a partner.

be	go	like	live	play	take

1. **Sara:** Mary, what _____ you interested in?

    Mary: Well, I _____ hiking on the weekends. And on Fridays,

    I _____ French lessons.

2. **Emma:** _____ your brother interested in sports?

    Mika: Yes, he _____. He _____ soccer a lot.

3. **Anna:** _____ your parents from China?

    Junko: No, they _____. They _____ from Japan, but they

    _____ in the United States now.

4. **Joe:** _____ you good at Scrabble? I _____ Scrabble a lot.

    Rob: No, I _____ good at Scrabble. But my brothers _____

    Scrabble often.

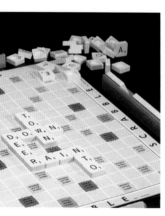

Scrabble™

D. COMPOSE Put the words in the correct order. Then ask and answer the questions with a partner.

1. you / where / people / do / usually meet

    _____

2. know / do / on your street / people / you

    _____

3. your / do / what / you do / with / friends

_____

4. you / go / friends / where / with / your / do

_____

iQ PRACTICE Go online for more practice with the simple present of *be* and other verbs. *Practice > Unit 1 > Activities 7–8*

PRONUNCIATION Simple present third-person *-s / -es*

There are three ways to pronounce the final *-s* or *-es* of a simple present verb.

/ s /	/ z /	/ ɪz /
gets makes	listens plays	watches washes

🔊 **A. IDENTIFY** Listen to the sentences. Circle the sound that you hear at the end of the verb. Then practice the sentences with a partner.

1. He goes shopping on Saturdays.	/ s /	/ z /	/ ɪz /
2. Khalid works downtown.	/ s /	/ z /	/ ɪz /
3. Sam plays video games in the evening.	/ s /	/ z /	/ ɪz /
4. Sun-Hee sometimes watches TV after work.	/ s /	/ z /	/ ɪz /
5. Mary gets together with friends on Sundays.	/ s /	/ z /	/ ɪz /
6. Mika lives in Los Angeles.	/ s /	/ z /	/ ɪz /
7. David washes his car on Saturdays.	/ s /	/ z /	/ ɪz /
8. Miteb belongs to a golf club.	/ s /	/ z /	/ ɪz /

David washes his car.

B. CREATE Write five sentences about your friends. Use verbs from the box.

belongs	gets	goes	plays	takes	washes	watches

1. _____

2. _____

3. _____

4. _____

5. _____

C. CATEGORIZE Read your sentences from Activity B to a partner. For each of your partner's sentences, circle the sound you hear.

| 1. / s /   / z /   / ɪz / | 3. / s /   / z /   / ɪz / | 5. / s /   / z /   / ɪz / |
| 2. / s /   / z /   / ɪz / | 4. / s /   / z /   / ɪz / | |

iQ PRACTICE   Go online for more practice with simple present third-person verbs ending in *-s* and *-es*. *Practice › Unit 1 › Activity 9*

SPEAKING SKILL *Part 1* **Keeping a conversation going**

Adding information

Short answers to questions do not help conversations. Give extra information to keep your conversation going.

Answer is too short.	Answer is good.
A: Rome is my favorite city. What's yours? B: **Shanghai.**	A: Rome is my favorite city. What's yours? B: **Shanghai. It has amazing buildings and delicious food!**
A: I like cooking. How about you? B: **I like cooking, too.**	A: I like cooking. How about you? B: **I like cooking, too. I often cook with friends on the weekends.**

TIP FOR SUCCESS

Ask short questions like *How about you?* or *What's yours?* to get the other person's opinion or answer.

A. CREATE Write answers to the questions. Add extra information. Then ask and answer the questions with a partner.

1. A: What are your hobbies?

   B: _____

2. A: I like soccer. How about you?

   B: _____

3. A: What are you good at?

   B: _____

4. A: *Great Expectations* is my favorite book. What's yours?

   B: _____

5. A: Are you interested in history?

   B: _____

6. A: I'm interested in cooking. How about you?

   B: _____

Taking time to think

Sometimes you can't answer a question right away. Use these special expressions before you answer. They tell people, "I am thinking."

🔊 ⌐ Hmm.   Let's see.   Let me see.   Let me think.   Uh …   Well …

🔊 **B. APPLY** Listen to the conversation. Complete the sentences with the expressions you hear. Then practice the conversation with a partner.

Tom: Carlos, what's your favorite sport?

Carlos: _____, it's soccer. But I also like basketball. What's yours?
       ₁

Tom: _____. It's probably volleyball. I play on the beach in the
     ₂
summer.

Carlos: Where's your favorite beach?

Tom: _____. Miami has a really good beach.
     ₃

Carlos: _____, what's your favorite beach near here?
       ₄

Tom: Ocean Beach is my favorite. It's beautiful! Do you know any beaches near here?

People surf at East Beach.

Carlos: _____. _____, I like East Beach. It has
       ₅   ₆
really big waves. People surf there.

C. EXTEND Work with a partner. Practice the questions and answers in Activity A on page 16 again. Use special expressions like *Hmm* and *Let me think.*

   A: *What are your hobbies?*
   B: *Let me think. I like games. I play Scrabble a lot.*

iQ PRACTICE Go online for more practice with keeping a conversation going.
Practice > Unit 1 > Activity 10

When you take notes, don't try to write down every word that you hear. Just write the important or meaningful words.

Read this sample from an interview.

Michael: What's your name?

Sung: My name is Sung-bo Shin. You can call me Sung.

Michael: Where are you from?

Sung: I'm from Seoul, South Korea.

Michael: Do you have a job?

Sung: Yes, I do. I'm a construction worker.

Michael: What are you interested in?

Sung: I like to swim and run. I also like to paint.

Look at the interviewer's notes. The interviewer only wrote the important words.

Sung-bo Shin (Sung)
Seoul, South Korea
construction worker
swimming, running, painting

UNIT ASSIGNMENT

OBJECTIVE ▶

Interview and introduce a classmate

In this assignment, you are going to interview a classmate and introduce him or her to the class. Think about the Unit Question, "What are you interested in?" Use the listening, the unit video, and your work in this unit. Look at the Self-Assessment checklist on page 20.

CONSIDER THE IDEAS

A. IDENTIFY What do you say in an introduction? Check (✓) the information.

☐ a greeting

☐ telephone number

☐ country

☐ job

☐ favorite book

☐ hobbies and interests

☐ name

B. IDENTIFY Listen to this sample introduction. Then look at the list in Activity A. What information is in the introduction? Circle the ideas in Activity A.

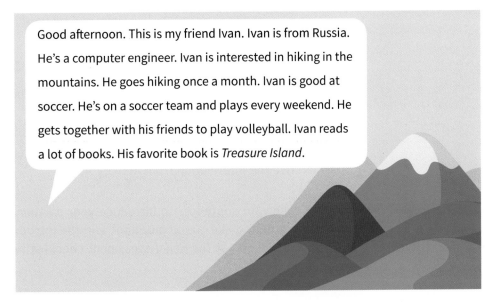

> Good afternoon. This is my friend Ivan. Ivan is from Russia. He's a computer engineer. Ivan is interested in hiking in the mountains. He goes hiking once a month. Ivan is good at soccer. He's on a soccer team and plays every weekend. He gets together with his friends to play volleyball. Ivan reads a lot of books. His favorite book is *Treasure Island*.

PREPARE AND SPEAK

A. FIND IDEAS Work with a partner. Follow these steps.

1. Add a question to the personal questionnaire below.

PERSONAL QUESTIONNAIRE

1. What's your name? _____

2. Where are you from? _____

3. What's your favorite book? _____

4. What's your favorite food? _____
   _____

5. What are your hobbies and interests? _____
   _____

6. What are you good at? _____
   _____

7. _____
   _____
   _____

2. Use the questions to interview your partner. Write your partner's answers in the questionnaire on page 19. Write only the important words.

3. When you answer the questions, give extra information (not just short answers). Use special expressions like *Hmm* and *Let me think*.

B. RESTATE Compare notes with your partner.

iQ PRACTICE Go online for more practice with writing important words. *Practice > Unit 1 > Activity 11*

C. ORGANIZE IDEAS Write three to five interesting sentences about your partner. Use the information from Activity A.

TIP FOR SUCCESS
In your presentation, speak clearly so your classmates can hear you. Look at the audience.

D. SPEAK Use your sentences to introduce your partner to the class. Include a greeting like "Good morning" and the introduction phrase "This is . . . ." Look at the Self-Assessment checklist below before you begin.

iQ PRACTICE Go online for your alternate Unit Assignment. *Practice > Unit 1 > Activity 12*

CHECK AND REFLECT

A. CHECK Think about the Unit Assignment as you complete the Self-Assessment checklist.

SELF-ASSESSMENT	Yes	No
My introduction was clear.	☐	☐
I used vocabulary from this unit.	☐	☐
I used the verb *be* and simple present statements correctly.	☐	☐
I included interesting information about my partner.	☐	☐
I took notes using only important words.	☐	☐

B. REFLECT Discuss these questions with a partner or group.

1. What is something new you learned in this unit?

2. Think about the Unit Question—What are you interested in? Is your answer different now than when you started this unit? If yes, how is it different? Why?

iQ PRACTICE Go to the online discussion board to discuss these questions. *Practice > Unit 1 > Activity 13*

TRACK YOUR SUCCESS

iQ PRACTICE Go online to check the words and phrases you have learned in this unit. *Practice › Unit 1 › Activity 14*

Check (✓) the skills you learned. If you need more work on a skill, refer to the page(s) in parentheses.

CRITICAL THINKING   ☐ I can notice similarities between things. (pp. 6–7)

VOCABULARY   ☐ I can understand collocations for hobbies and interests. (p. 8)

GRAMMAR   ☐ I can use the simple present of *be* and other verbs. (pp. 12, 13–14)

PRONUNCIATION   ☐ I can pronounce simple present third-person *-s / -es*. (p. 15)

SPEAKING   ☐ I can keep a conversation going. (pp. 16, 17)

NOTE-TAKING   ☐ I can write important words when taking notes. (p. 18)

OBJECTIVE ▶   ☐ I can use information and ideas to interview a classmate and introduce him or her to the class.

Education

2

What makes a good school?

A. Discuss these questions with your classmates.

1. How many students go to your school?

2. Does your school have any clubs or sports teams?

3. Look at the photo. Does your school have places like this one? What do students do there?

B. Listen to *The Q Classroom* online. Then answer these questions.

1. What did the students say? What does each student like in a school?

2. Who do you agree with? Which ideas are less important to you?

C. What do you want in a school? Complete the chart below. Check (✓) the correct column for each item.

	Very important	Important	Not important
sports	☐	☐	☐
clubs	☐	☐	☐
friends	☐	☐	☐
interesting classes	☐	☐	☐
sunny weather	☐	☐	☐
your own idea: _____	☐	☐	☐

iQ PRACTICE Go to the online discussion board to discuss the Unit Question with your classmates. *Practice > Unit 2 > Activity 1*

UNIT OBJECTIVE

Listen to a conversation. Use information and ideas to give a presentation about a perfect school.

23

LISTENING

OBJECTIVE ▶

Asking Questions about a University

You are going to listen to someone describe a university. Think about what makes a good school.

PREVIEW THE LISTENING

A. VOCABULARY Here are some words and phrases from the listening. Read the definitions. Then read the sentences. Which explanation is correct? Circle *a* or *b*.

campus *(noun)* ⚲ the buildings of a university or college and the land around them

community *(noun)* ⚲ OPAL all the people who live in a place

download *(verb)* ⚲ to get data from another computer, usually using the Internet

foreign language *(noun phrase)* ⚲ words that people from a different country say and write

online *(adjective, adverb)* ⚲ OPAL being connected to a computer or the Internet

professor *(noun)* ⚲ a teacher at a college or university

skill *(noun)* ⚲ OPAL the ability to do something well

special *(adjective)* ⚲ not ordinary or usual; different from what is normal

⚲ Oxford 3000™ words   OPAL Oxford Phrasal Academic Lexicon

1. My university has a big **campus**. It has more than 100 buildings.

   a. The classrooms are part of the campus.

   b. The students are part of the campus.

2. Sultan can't go **online** in his room. He goes to a cafe to check his email.

   a. Sultan can go on the Internet in his room.

   b. Sultan can't go on the Internet in his room.

3. Maryam has a great math **professor**. His classes are always interesting.

   a. A professor is a university student.

   b. A professor is a university teacher.

4. John gets good grades, so he is in **special** classes. His classes are difficult.

   a. John's classes are different or unusual.

   b. John's classes are normal or regular.

5. Ali can't **download** his email because he can't go online.

   a. Ali can't get his email.

   b. Ali has a lot of email.

6. Writing is an important **skill**. Huda writes every day. She wants to be a good writer.

   a. Playing tennis is also a skill.

   b. Watching television is also a skill.

7. David is from France. For David, Korean is a **foreign language**.

   a. French is also a foreign language for David.

   b. Spanish is also a foreign language for David.

8. A **community** is a group of people. They live or work in the same area.

   a. A bus stop is a kind of community.

   b. A town is a kind of community.

B. APPLY Complete the sentences with words and phrases from Activity A.

TIP FOR SUCCESS
The word *school* can refer to any educational institute. The words *college* and *university* often have the same meaning: a place of higher education with degree programs.

1. At my school, all the students study a _____. I'm in a Japanese class.

2. Fahad's university has a really small _____. You can walk across it in ten minutes.

3. A class is a kind of _____. The teachers and students work together.

4. I have to talk to my biology _____. I have a question about the test.

5. My brother _____ a lot of books from the Internet. He reads them on his phone or on his tablet.

6. Reading is an important _____. Good students read well.

iQ PRACTICE   Go online for more practice with the vocabulary.
Practice > Unit 2 > Activities 2–3

C. PREVIEW You are going to listen to two people talk about Al Jaser Online University. What do you think you can do at an online university? Check (✓) your answers.

☐ be part of a community ☐ play sports

☐ live in a dormitory ☐ watch lectures

☐ get books from a library ☐ eat in a dining hall

☐ meet other students ☐ take classes at any time

D. IDENTIFY Read the questions. Circle *Yes* or *No*.

1. Does your school have a library?	Yes	No
2. Does it have a dormitory?	Yes	No
3. Does it have Internet access?	Yes	No

E. CREATE What are some other things at your school?

_____

_____

WORK WITH THE LISTENING

A. CATEGORIZE Read the sentences. Listen to the conversation. Write *T* (true) or *F* (false). Then correct the false statements.

iQ RESOURCES   Go online to download extra vocabulary support.
Resources > Extra Vocabulary > Unit 2

____ 1. The classes are online.

_____

____ 2. The university has a campus.

_____

____ 3. Students can practice foreign languages with other students.

_____

____ 4. The school has about 2,000 students.

_____

_____ 5. All the students live in the Middle East.

_____

_____ 6. The professors live all over the world.

_____

B. IDENTIFY Read the questions. Then circle the correct answer.

1. Who is Sarah?

    a. an employee at Al Jaser Online University

    b. a student at Al Jaser Online University

    c. a new student

2. Why does Layla call?

    a. She is a new student.

    b. She wants information about the school.

    c. She wants a job.

3. What is special about this university?

    a. Students can only study a few subjects.

    b. Students come from many different countries.

    c. It's small, so you can talk to your professors every day.

iQ PRACTICE Go online for additional listening and comprehension.
Practice > Unit 2 > Activity 4

LISTENING SKILL Listening for examples

People give examples with *like*. *Like* comes in the middle of a sentence.

    I study in different places, **like** the library or my dormitory.

People also give examples with *for example*. *For example* can come at the beginning of a sentence.

    Watson University has many interesting classes. **For example**, I have classes in French and history.

IDENTIFY Listen again to the conversation about Al Jaser Online University. Listen for examples with *for example* or *like*. Circle the correct answer.

1. What can you talk about in a chat room at Al Jaser Online University?

    a. science   c. sports

    b. math   d. history

2. What else can you do in a chat room at Al Jaser?

   a. talk with professors   c. practice French

   b. talk about tests   d. watch lectures

3. At Al Jaser Online University, you can join a club. What examples does Sarah give?

   a. book club and math club   c. science club and math club

   b. French club and science club   d. science club and book club

4. Where do some of the professors live?

   a. Japan and England   c. England, Saudi Arabia, and France

   b. France and Canada   d. Saudi Arabia, France, and Japan

5. What kinds of classes can students take at Al Jaser?

   a. history, math, and science

   b. foreign languages, history, and sports

   c. math, computers, and science

   d. history, art, and music

iQ PRACTICE Go online for more practice with listening for examples.
Practice > Unit 2 > Activity 5

NOTE-TAKING SKILL Taking notes on examples

 It is good to write down examples. Writing them in a chart helps you remember them. Listen to two students talk about a college. Then look at the chart below. It shows examples of things the students talk about.

Mosa's college		
Classes	**Sports teams**	**Clubs**
history	tennis	book
math	soccer	hiking
	baseball	

🔊 **CATEGORIZE** Listen again to part of the conversation about Al Jaser Online University. Work with a partner to complete the chart with examples.

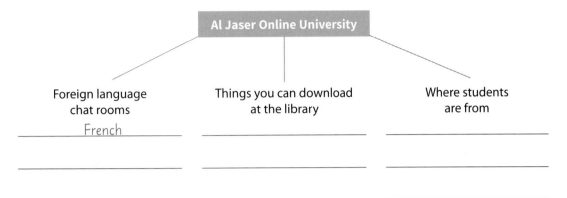

Al Jaser Online University

Foreign language chat rooms	Things you can download at the library	Where students are from
French		

iQ PRACTICE Go online for more practice with taking notes on examples.
Practice ▸ Unit 2 ▸ Activity 6

BUILDING VOCABULARY Using the dictionary: antonyms

Antonyms are words with opposite meanings. For example, *good* and *bad* are antonyms. Most forms of words—nouns, verbs, adjectives, adverbs, and prepositions—can have antonyms.

The dictionary often gives antonyms in the definition of a word. In the example below, notice the antonyms of *hard*.

> **hard**[1] ⚲ /hard/ *adjective* (hard·er, hard·est)
> **1** not soft: *These apples are very hard.* ◆ *I couldn't sleep because the bed was too hard.* ⊃ **ANTONYM soft**
> **2** difficult to do or understand: *The exam was very hard.* ◆ *hard work* ⊃ **ANTONYM easy**
> **3** full of problems: *He's had **a hard life**.* ⊃ **ANTONYM easy**
> **4** not kind or gentle: *She is very **hard on** her children.* ⊃ **ANTONYM soft**

All dictionary entries adapted from the *Oxford Basic American Dictionary for learners of English* © Oxford University Press 2011.

A. APPLY Write an antonym for each word. Use the words in the box.
Use your dictionary to help you.

above	cheap	easy	strength
badly	complicated	negative	succeed

1. hard _____

2. fail _____

3. below _____

4. weakness _____

5. positive _____

6. simple _____

7. expensive _____

8. well _____

B. IDENTIFY Read the sentences. Circle the correct answer.

1. Min-seo doesn't like her school. The classrooms are always (clean / dirty).

2. In my history class, we have many discussions and presentations.
   I like it a lot. It's very (interesting / boring).

3. One (strength / weakness) of my school is the library. It's very small, and it
   doesn't have a lot of books.

4. The school is in a (safe / dangerous) part of town. Don't go out late at night.

5. My school costs a lot of money. It's very (cheap / expensive).

6. In a good school, all the students (fail / succeed).

7. Sarah lives (on / off) campus. Her dormitory is near the library.

8. My math class is really (easy / hard). I know all the answers.

C. COMPOSE Choose three adjectives. Write a sentence for each adjective
and its antonym.

My chemistry class is <u>hard</u>.   Math is <u>easy</u> for me.

_____

_____

_____

_____

_____

_____

dormitory room

iQ PRACTICE Go online for more practice with using the dictionary.
Practice > Unit 2 > Activity 7

WORK WITH THE VIDEO

A. PREVIEW What is hard about going to a new school?

VIDEO VOCABULARY

originally (adv.) in the beginning

actually (adv.) really; in fact

basically (adv.) in the most important ways

hand in hand (phr.) closely connected

homemade (adj.) made at home, not bought at a store

iQ RESOURCES Go online to watch the video about school in Japan.
Resources > Video > Unit 2 > Unit Video

B. CATEGORIZE Watch the video two or three times. Take notes in the first part of the chart.

	Things Sophie liked about her Japanese high school	My opinion about those things
Notes from the video		
My ideas		

C. EXTEND Do you like the same things Sophie liked? Write *Agree* or *Disagree* in the chart above. What are some ways the Japanese school is different from your school? Write your ideas in the chart above.

SAY WHAT YOU THINK

SYNTHESIZE Think about the listening and the unit video as you discuss the questions.

1. Which kind of school do you like better? Why?

2. What are some good things about each school?

3. How important is it to meet with other students and teachers in person? Why?

SPEAKING

OBJECTIVE ▶ At the end of this unit, you are going to give a group presentation about a perfect school.

GRAMMAR Adjectives; Adverbs + adjectives

Adjectives

1. Adjectives describe nouns (people, places, things, or ideas).

   • An adjective can come after the verb *be*. It describes the subject.

subject	*be*	adjective
The school	is	**large.**
The students	are	**smart.**

   • An adjective can come before a noun. It describes the noun.

	adjective	noun
It's a	**safe**	**school.**
I have	**good**	**classes.**

2. There are no singular or plural adjectives.
   - ✓ Correct: They are **interesting classes**.
   - ✗ Incorrect: They are interestings classes.

3. Do not use an article (*the*, *a*, or *an*) before an adjective with no noun.
   - ✓ Correct: The class is **interesting**.
   - ✗ Incorrect: The class is an interesting.

Adverbs + adjectives

1. Adverbs make adjectives stronger.
   - It's a **pretty** interesting class.   It's a **very** safe school.
   - That school is **really** safe!   This classroom is **extremely** noisy!

   • Use *pretty* in speaking and informal writing. Don't use it in papers for your classes.

2. You can use *pretty*, *really*, *very*, and *extremely* before:
   - an adjective alone: That school is **really excellent**.
   - an adjective + a noun: It's a **very active class**.

iQ RESOURCES Go online to watch the Grammar Skill Video.
Resources > Video > Unit 2 > Grammar Skill Video

A. IDENTIFY Read the paragraph. Find the ten adjective and adverb errors and correct them.

> new university
> Well, I am now at my ~~university new~~. It's in a large very city. It's pretty different from our small town. It's an extremely noisy, but I love it. There are excellents museums and parks. I live in an apartment expensive in the city. The building is beautiful really, but it's pretty old. My school is great, but my classes are big extremely. Some of my classes have 200 people in them! But my professors are a very good, and my classes are really interesting. We have a science laboratory great. I study biology there. Also, the people here are friendly very, but I miss my old friends.

B. COMPOSE Complete the conversation with adjectives or adverbs + adjectives. Use your own ideas. Then practice with a partner.

A: Do you like this school?

B: Yes, I do. I think that it's a _____ _____ school. What do you think?

A: I like it, too. The teachers are _____, and the classes are _____.

B: What do you think of the library?

A: I think that it's _____ _____. What do you think of the campus?

B: I think that it's _____ _____.

a university library

iQ PRACTICE Go online for more practice with adjectives and adverbs + adjectives. *Practice > Unit 2 > Activity 8*

iQ PRACTICE Go online for the Grammar Expansion: adverbs of degree and the adverb *too*. *Practice > Unit 2 > Activity 9*

PRONUNCIATION Sentence stress

When you speak, you **stress** certain **important words**. This means you say them a little more loudly.

Important words—like nouns, adjectives, and adverbs—give the information in the sentences.

You do not usually stress words like pronouns, prepositions, *a / an / the*, the verb *be*, or the verb *do*.

🔊
> There are **two sports fields**.
> The **museum** is **not interesting**.
> We **go** to **school** in a **really dangerous neighborhood**.
> Do you **have** a **class today**?

🔊 **A. IDENTIFY** <u>Underline</u> the stressed words. Listen and check your answers. Then practice the sentences with a partner.

1. Does the school have a fencing team?

2. I have two classes in the morning.

3. We want a safe and clean school.

4. The college is in a dangerous city.

5. The coffee shops have free Internet access.

6. What is a good school?

7. Our sports field is pretty big.

8. My school is really great!

B. COMPOSE Write five sentences about your school. Use adjectives and the adverbs *pretty, really, very,* and *extremely*.

C. IDENTIFY Work with a partner. Read each other's sentences. Underline the stressed words. Then practice the sentences.

fencing

The <u>campus</u> is <u>extremely</u> <u>large</u>.

iQ PRACTICE Go online for more practice with sentence stress. *Practice > Unit 2 > Activity 10*

SPEAKING SKILL Giving opinions

An **opinion** is something that a person thinks or feels. Use the phrases
I think that . . . and *In my opinion, . . .* to give an opinion.

> **I think that** students need computers.
> **In my opinion,** small classes are important.

You can answer opinions with *I agree* or *I disagree* followed by your opinion.

> A: **I think that** our school is great.
> B: **I agree.** I think that the classes are interesting.
> C: **I disagree.** In my opinion, the classes are too big.

A. IDENTIFY Listen and complete the conversations. Use expressions from the box above. Compare your answers with a partner.

ACADEMIC LANGUAGE

The corpus shows that *I think that* is a common phrase in academic speaking.

⌐_____ OPAL
Oxford Phrasal Academic Lexicon

1. A: _____ a good school gives a lot of tests.

   Then students study every day.

   B: _____. Class discussions make students study.

2. A: _____ sports are really important. Students need

   healthy bodies.

   B: _____. Exercise is very important.

TIP FOR SUCCESS

When you write *In my opinion*, use a comma after it. Don't use a comma after *I think that*.

3. A: _____ the food in our dining hall isn't very good. I don't

   like it!

   B: _____. _____ it tastes terrible. I usually cook

   my own food.

4. A: Our school isn't in a good neighborhood. _____ it's very

   dangerous. I hear police sirens all the time.

   B: _____. You hear sirens because the police station is on the

   same street! _____ the school is very safe.

B. CREATE Write answers to the questions. Start your answers with *I think that* or *In my opinion*. Then ask and answer the questions with a partner.

1. What is the perfect number of students in a foreign language class?

2. In your opinion, what makes a class interesting? Give two ideas.

3. Do you think it's better to work alone or with a group? Why?

iQ PRACTICE Go online for more practice with giving your opinion.
Practice > Unit 2 > Activity 11

CRITICAL THINKING STRATEGY

Giving reasons for opinions

It is not enough to say your opinion. Explain *why* you think so. Give reasons for your opinion to make it stronger. Ask yourself *why*.

Opinion	Reason (*Why?*)
I think that it's important to have good friends at school.	Good friends can support me and help me study.
It's not important to have good friends at school.	It's more difficult to study with my friends because we chat a lot.

iQ PRACTICE Go online to watch the Critical Thinking Video and check your comprehension. *Practice > Unit 2 > Activity 12*

C. EVALUATE Give your opinion of the following statements. Circle *Yes* or *No*. Think about the reasons for your opinion.

WHAT MAKES A GOOD SCHOOL AND A GOOD EDUCATIONAL EXPERIENCE?

1. Yes No It's important to learn a foreign language in school.
2. Yes No It's important to have good friends at school.
3. Yes No Every school needs a lot of clubs and teams.
4. Yes No A good school has computers for students to use.
5. Yes No Every campus needs a library and a sports field.
6. Yes No Good schools have small classes.
7. Yes No A good school has a large campus.
8. Yes No A good school is a community.
9. Yes No A good school has new buildings.
10. Yes No Good schools are always in big cities.
11. Yes No In good schools, students can talk to teachers outside of class.
12. Yes No In a good class, students can ask the teacher questions.

D. DISCUSS Discuss your answers with a partner. Give reasons for your opinions. Use *I think that* and *In my opinion* to give your opinions.

Plan a perfect school

OBJECTIVE ▶

In this assignment, you are going to plan a perfect school. This can be a high school, university, or other kind of school. Then you are going to present your plan to the class. Think about the Unit Question, "What makes a good school?" Use the listening, the unit video, and your work in this unit. Look at the Self-Assessment checklist on page 38.

CONSIDER THE IDEAS

IDENTIFY Listen to a group present their ideas for a perfect school. Check (✓) the ideas that they give. Then compare answers with a partner.

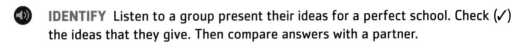

☐ 1. The perfect school is large.

☐ 2. The classes are very small.

☐ 3. The school has a lot of clubs, like a book club and a soccer club.

☐ 4. There is a big gym.

☐ 5. Students get free computers.

☐ 6. The school is in a big city.

☐ 7. Apartments in town are cheap and beautiful.

☐ 8. Food on campus is cheap.

PREPARE AND SPEAK

TIP FOR SUCCESS

Examples can make your opinion strong and clear: *I think that a good school needs a sports field, like a soccer field. Students need exercise. It makes them healthy.*

A. FIND IDEAS Work with a group. Write answers for these questions. Use *I think that* and *In my opinion* to share your ideas. Give a reason for each opinion.

1. Is your perfect school big or small? How many students are in a class?

2. What does the school have? For example, does it have a swimming pool? Does it have computers?

3. Is your school in a big city or a small town? What can students do there?

4. What is special about your school? How is it different from other schools?

B. ORGANIZE IDEAS Work with your group. Prepare your presentation.

1. Each group member chooses at least one question from Activity A.

2. Write your part of the presentation. Include at least one example or reason for your idea.

3. First speaker: Use these sentences as your introduction.

   Good (morning / afternoon / evening). Today we are presenting our plan for the perfect school.

4. Last speaker: Use these sentences as your conclusion.

   That's the end of our presentation. Thank you. Do you have any questions?

C. SPEAK Present your ideas to your class. Look at the Self-Assessment checklist below before you begin.

iQ PRACTICE Go online for your alternate Unit Assignment.
Practice > Unit 2 > Activity 13

CHECK AND REFLECT

A. CHECK Think about the Unit Assignment as you complete the Self-Assessment checklist.

SELF-ASSESSMENT	Yes	No
I gave my opinion clearly.	☐	☐
I gave a reason for my opinion.	☐	☐
I used vocabulary from this unit.	☐	☐
I used adjectives and adverbs + adjectives correctly.	☐	☐
I stressed words in sentences correctly.	☐	☐

B. REFLECT Discuss these questions with a partner or group.

1. What is something new you learned in this unit?

2. Think about the Unit Question—What makes a good school? Is your answer different now than when you started this unit? If yes, how is it different? Why?

iQ PRACTICE Go to the online discussion board to discuss these questions.
Practice > Unit 2 > Activity 14

TRACK YOUR SUCCESS

iQ PRACTICE Go online to check the words and phrases you have learned in this unit. *Practice > Unit 2 > Activity 15*

Check (✓) the skills you learned. If you need more work on a skill, refer to the page(s) in parentheses.

LISTENING	☐ I can identify examples. (p. 27)
NOTE-TAKING	☐ I can take notes on examples. (p. 28)
VOCABULARY	☐ I can use the dictionary to understand antonyms. (p. 29)
GRAMMAR	☐ I can use adjectives and adverbs + adjectives. (p. 32)
PRONUNCIATION	☐ I can stress important words. (p. 34)
SPEAKING	☐ I can give my opinion. (p. 35)
CRITICAL THINKING	☐ I can give reasons for my opinion. (p. 36)
OBJECTIVE ▶	☐ I can use information and ideas to present a plan about a perfect school.

3

Cultural Studies

How do you choose your food?

A. Discuss these questions with your classmates.

1. Circle the adjectives that describe food. Compare with a partner.

active	delicious	healthy	sour
close	difficult	important	spicy
dangerous	fresh	salty	sweet

2. What kind of food do you like to eat? Where do you get it?

3. Look at the photo. Where do you think these people get their food?

B. Listen to *The Q Classroom* online. Then answer these questions.

1. What did the students say about the foods they like?

2. Which student likes spicy food? Who doesn't eat much sugar? Who likes convenience?

3. Which student is similar to you in food tastes? For example, do you like spicy food? Why or why not?

iQ PRACTICE   Go to the online discussion board to discuss the Unit Question with your classmates. *Practice > Unit 3 > Activity 1*

UNIT OBJECTIVE

Listen to a podcast. Use information and ideas to design a survey and interview a classmate.

LISTENING

Lifestyles and Food Choices

OBJECTIVE ▶

You are going to listen to a podcast about healthy food choices. Think about what makes food healthy.

PREVIEW THE LISTENING

A. VOCABULARY Here are some words from the listening. Read the definitions. Then complete the sentences below.

ACADEMIC LANGUAGE

Avoid is one of the most common words used in academic speaking and writing.

─────────── OPAL

Oxford Phrasal Academic Lexicon

---

avoid *(verb)* 🔑 OPAL to try not to do something; to stay away from something

flavor *(noun)* 🔑 the taste of food, like salty or sweet

ingredient *(noun)* 🔑 one of the things that are used to make food

memory *(noun)* 🔑 the ability to remember things

nutritious *(adjective)* good for you

organic *(adjective)* natural; organic food has only natural ingredients

vegetarian *(noun)* a person who does not eat meat

🔑 Oxford 3000™ words   **OPAL** Oxford Phrasal Academic Lexicon

1. I put tomato sauce, garlic, cheese, and onions in my pasta. It has a lot of
   _____.

2. Fruits are _____. For example, oranges have vitamin C.

3. Amir has a good _____ for faces. He remembers everyone he sees.

4. Amanda and Matt _____ food with a lot of fat. For example, they don't eat French fries or cheeseburgers.

5. Lemons are sour, but oranges have a sweet _____.

6. Sam doesn't eat chicken or beef. He's a _____.

7. John buys his food at a health-food store. He eats only _____ food.

TIP FOR SUCCESS

Artificial means not natural or real. Some food has artificial ingredients. These are made by people.

B. Answer the questions. Then compare with a partner.

1. What is an example of a food with a strong flavor? _____

2. Are you a vegetarian or do you eat meat? _____

3. How often do you eat organic food? _____

4. Do you avoid food with artificial ingredients? _____
   Why or why not? _____

5. Name three foods that are very nutritious. _____
   _____

iQ PRACTICE Go online for more practice with the vocabulary.
Practice > Unit 3 > Activities 2–3

C. PREVIEW You are going to listen to a podcast about healthy food choices. Look at the pictures. Check (✓) the kinds of food you eat. How healthy are they? Write 1 (not healthy), 2 (a little healthy), or 3 (very healthy).

☐ meat ____

☐ vegetables ____

☐ fruit ____

☐ dessert ____

☐ dairy ____

☐ grains ____

Speakers use reasons to explain their actions. In conversations, speakers often use **why** to ask for reasons. They use **because** to give reasons.

A: **Why** do you eat sugar-free food?   A: **Why** don't you eat fast food?

B: **Because** sugar is bad for your teeth.   B: **Because** it has artificial
                                                  ingredients in it.

Listen for these two key words—*why* and *because*—to understand reasons.

A. IDENTIFY Read the sentences. Then listen to the conversations. Circle the correct answer.

1. Why does John buy only organic apples?

   a. Because they are cheap.

   b. Because they're good for him.

   c. Because he likes the flavor.

   d. Because they're sweet.

2. Why does Amanda avoid fattening foods?

   a. Because she doesn't like them.

   b. Because she wants to lose weight.

   c. Because they're bad for her health.

   d. Because she's allergic.

fattening foods

3. Why does James want to go out for dinner?

   a. Because his friend is a terrible cook.

   b. Because he is a terrible cook.

   c. Because it's cheap.

   d. Because he doesn't have any food at home.

4. Kay's Kitchen is Anna's favorite restaurant. Why?

   a. Because it's near her house.

   b. Because their food is delicious.

   c. Because their food is cheap.

   d. Because it's organic.

B. EXPLAIN Are you similar to John, Amanda, James, or Anna? Tell your classmates.

I think I'm similar to John. We both like organic food.

iQ PRACTICE Go online for more practice with listening for reasons.
Practice > Unit 3 > Activity 4

WORK WITH THE LISTENING

A. CATEGORIZE Listen to the podcast about berries. Read the statements. Write *T* (true) or *F* (false). Then correct the false statements.

iQ RESOURCES Go online to download extra vocabulary support.
Resources > Extra Vocabulary > Unit 3

____ 1. Brown and red foods have special chemicals that help you stay healthy.

_____

____ 2. Scientists studied people who ate berries.

_____

____ 3. Eating blueberries and strawberries helped the people remember more.

_____

____ 4. All fruits and vegetables are nutritious in the same way.

_____

____ 5. Melons and spinach help keep your stomach healthy.

_____

____ 6. If you don't eat meat, you can eat beans and whole grains like brown rice.

_____

B. APPLY Listen again. Circle the correct answer.

1. How many people did the researchers study?

   a. 16,000

   b. 1,600

   c. 160

2. What are other red or blue foods Anya talks about?

   a. beans, tomatoes, and beets

   b. melons, tomatoes, and meat

   c. cherries, peppers, and beans

3. What other color foods are healthy?

   a. green and purple

   b. white and pink

   c. orange and green

4. Why should you eat organic fruits and vegetables?

   a. They taste better.

   b. They are more nutritious.

   c. They are better for the environment.

5. What does Anya suggest you put on a sandwich?

   a. spinach

   b. tomatoes

   c. cheese

 CRITICAL THINKING STRATEGY

Recognizing cause and effect

Speakers often describe cause and effect relationships. A **cause** is like a reason. It can make something happen—which is the **effect**. An effect is an outcome or result.

The words and phrases *because*, *because of*, and *since* can introduce a cause. The word *so* introduces an effect. Verbs like *help*, *cause*, and *give* can introduce effects, too.

Other cause-effect relationships are not stated as directly. Think about the relationship between the two things. The cause can come first or second in the sentence.

Cause	Effect
Because I love animals,	I don't eat meat.
I love animals,	**so** I don't eat meat.
Dairy products	**help** build strong bones.

Sometimes the effect of one action is also the cause of another.

   cause   →   effect and cause   →   effect

   Because I love animals, I don't eat meat, so I eat whole grains, beans, and nuts instead.

iQ PRACTICE Go online to watch the Critical Thinking Video and check your comprehension. *Practice > Unit 3 > Activity 5*

C. ANALYZE Listen again. Match the cause with its effect.

Cause

1. special chemicals that give food red and blue color ____
2. eating more berries ____
3. the results of the research ____
4. orange and green foods ____
5. being a vegetarian ____
6. using fruits and vegetables as ingredients ____

Effect

a. get the same health benefits
b. decision to eat berries every day
c. better memories
d. help keep us healthy, and keep our brains in good shape
e. keep your heart healthy
f. eat a lot of fruits and vegetables

D. RESTATE Answer the questions.

1. Why should we eat berries? _____

2. What happened in the study? _____

_____

3. What foods are part of a healthy diet according to Anya?

_____

iQ PRACTICE Go online to listen to *Breakfast in Different Countries* and check your comprehension. *Practice > Unit 3 > Activity 6*

A **prefix** comes at the beginning of a word. It changes the meaning of the word. A **suffix** comes at the end of a word. It often changes the part of speech. Learners' dictionaries usually give definitions for prefixes and suffixes. Other dictionaries often list them at the back.

The prefixes *non-* and *un-* mean "not." The suffix *-free* means "without," and it changes a noun (*sugar*) into an adjective (*sugar-free*). Look at the definitions.

Prefix
non- not: ***non*fiction** (= *writing that is about real people, events*) ♦ *a **non**stop flight*

Suffix
-free (in adjectives) not containing the (usually bad) thing mentioned: *sugar-**free** cola* ♦ *fat-**free** yogurt* ♦ *a smoke-**free** environment* ♦ *a tax-**free** savings account*

Prefix
un- not; the opposite of: ***un*happy** ♦ ***un*true** (= *not true*) ♦ ***un*lock** ♦ ***un*dress** (= *to take clothes off*)

All dictionary entries adapted from the *Oxford Basic American Dictionary for learners of English* © Oxford University Press 2011.

A. APPLY Complete each sentence with a word from the box.

nondairy	salt-free	unfriendly	unsafe
nonfat	sugar-free	unhealthy	unusual

☐ 1. I worry about foods with a lot of fat. I drink only _____ milk.

☐ 2. I eat a lot of junk food, like chips, cookies, and cake. I never exercise. I'm often sick. I'm very _____.

☐ 3. She doesn't talk to anyone. She's very _____.

☐ 4. I'm allergic to food with milk, cheese, or butter. I eat only _____ food.

☐ 5. I don't eat food with a lot of salt in it. Salt is bad for my health. I try to eat _____ food.

☐ 6. I only eat organic food. I think food with artificial ingredients is _____.

☐ 7. I avoid food and drinks with sugar. I try to have only _____ food and drinks.

☐ 8. I like to try _____ foods. I don't like to eat the same kind of food every day.

I'm allergic to food with milk.

OIL SHORTENING (PARTIALLY
D SOYBEAN OIL, PROPYLENE
AND DIESTERS OF FATS, MC
ERIDES). CONTAINS 2% OR
NG (SODIUM BICARBONATE
M PHOSPHATE), DEXTROSE, M
TARCH, SALT, CELLULOSE GU
RIN, ARTIFICIAL FLAVORS, (
YELLOW 5 LAKE, RED 40 LAK

artificial ingredients

B. IDENTIFY Check (✓) the items in Activity A that are true for you. Then compare your answers with a partner.

C. EXTEND Find two more prefixes or suffixes in your dictionary. Write three sentences with those words that have those prefixes or suffixes.

iQ PRACTICE Go online for more practice with prefixes and suffixes. *Practice > Unit 3 > Activity 7*

PRONUNCIATION Stressed syllables

In words with two or more syllables, you usually **stress one syllable**. You say the syllable with more energy. In these words, the bold syllables are stressed.

or • **gan** • ic   veg • e • **tar** • i • an   un • **friend** • ly

A. IDENTIFY Listen to the words. Circle the stressed syllables. Then practice with a partner.

1. de • li • cious
2. al • ler • gic
3. un • health • y
4. ed • u • ca • tion
5. in • gre • di • ent

6. sug • ar • free
7. gar • den
8. din • ner
9. non • dai • ry
10. com • mu • ni • ty

B. APPLY Listen to the sentences. Circle the stressed syllables in words with two or more syllables.

TIP FOR SUCCESS
We usually don't stress words like pronouns, prepositions, and articles. See the Pronunciation box on page 34 for more information.

1. In my opinion, artificial ingredients are unsafe.
2. He doesn't eat chicken or beef.
3. He wants to lose weight, so he's on a diet.
4. This soup has an unusual flavor.
5. Are these cookies sugar-free?
6. She grows organic tomatoes in her garden.

C. EXTEND Listen again. Underline the stressed words in the sentences.

iQ PRACTICE Go online for more practice with stressed syllables. *Practice > Unit 3 > Activity 8*

WORK WITH THE VIDEO

A. PREVIEW Do you like to buy food at farmers' markets? Why? Why not?

VIDEO VOCABULARY

fresh (adj.) made or picked recently

local (adj.) from a place near you

crisp (adj.) firm and fresh

juicy (adj.) full of juice

iQ RESOURCES Go online to watch the video about shopping at a farmers' market. *Resources > Video > Unit 3 > Unit Video*

B. CATEGORIZE Watch the video two or three times. Take notes in the first part of the chart.

	Things Jean wants to buy	Things she doesn't need to buy
Notes from the video		
My ideas		

C. EXTEND What are other things you can buy at a farmers' market? What are things you can't usually buy at a farmers' market? Write your ideas in the chart above.

? SAY WHAT YOU THINK

A. COMPOSE Think about the listening and the unit video. Answer these questions.

Food Survey

1. Do you eat meat? Why or why not?

   _____

   _____

2. Do you eat fast food? Why or why not?

   _____

3. Do you eat organic food? Why or why not?

   _____

4. Do you eat food with artificial ingredients? Why or why not?

   _____

5. What kinds of food do you usually eat? Why do you choose them?

   _____

   _____

6. What's your favorite food? Why?

   _____

7. What kinds of food do you avoid? Why?

   _____

   _____

8. What do you usually eat for breakfast?

   _____

TIP FOR SUCCESS

You can use *Why **don't** you . . . ?* or *Why **doesn't** he / she . . . ?* to ask why someone *doesn't* do something.

B. DISCUSS Discuss your answers with a partner.

A: *Do you eat meat?*

B: *Yes, I do.*

A: *Why?*

B: *Because it's delicious and I like the flavor.*

SPEAKING

OBJECTIVE ▶

At the end of this unit, you are going to design a survey about food and interview a classmate.

GRAMMAR Verbs + gerunds or infinitives

1. Gerunds and infinitives are usually words for activities.

    • A gerund is a **base verb + -ing**: *eating, cooking, baking.*

    • An infinitive is *to* + a **base verb**: *to eat, to cook, to bake.*

2. **Verbs + gerunds** You can use gerunds after these verbs.

subject	verb	gerund
We	**enjoy**	**cooking.**
I	**avoid**	**buying** fast food.

3. **Verbs + infinitives** You can use infinitives after these verbs.

subject	verb	infinitive
He	**tries**	**to eat** only organic food.
We	**need**	**to make** dinner.
They	**want**	**to eat** only healthy food.

4. **Verbs + gerunds *or* infinitives** You can use gerunds or infinitives after these verbs.

subject	verb	gerund or infinitive
He	**likes**	**to eat** at home. **eating** at home.
We	**hate**	**to shop** at Bob's Market. **shopping** at Bob's Market.
They	**love**	**to go out** to dinner. **going out** to dinner.
I	**can't stand**	**to cook.** **cooking.**

iQ RESOURCES Go online to watch the Grammar Skill Video.
Resources ❯ Video ❯ Unit 3 ❯ Grammar Skill Video

A. IDENTIFY Listen to the sentences. What do you hear? Circle the gerund or infinitive.

1. to cook / cooking
2. to eat / eating
3. to shop / shopping
4. to buy / buying
5. to eat / eating

6. to avoid / avoiding
7. to cook / cooking
8. to eat / eating
9. to eat / eating
10. to go / going

B. APPLY Complete the conversation with the correct infinitive or gerund forms. In some sentences, both a gerund and an infinitive are correct.

Mary: Sun-Hee, I have to make dinner for my husband's parents on Friday night. I'm so nervous. Can you help me?

Sun-Hee: Sure, I love _____ (cook). What kinds of food do they like
                                    1
_____ (eat)?
       2

Mary: Well, my mother-in-law enjoys _____ (try) new things,
                                                        3
but my father-in-law avoids _____ (eat) a lot of different things.
                                          4
For example, he's allergic to dairy foods, and he tries _____ (avoid) foods
                                                                        5
with a lot of salt.

Sun-Hee: What do they like?

Mary: Um, they like chicken and fish. And they like vegetables.

Sun-Hee: All right. I have a great recipe for roast chicken and vegetables.
It's spicy, but it's not very salty.

Mary: That sounds perfect! Thanks so much. I try _____ (cook), but I'm
                                                                  6
not very good in the kitchen.

Sun-Hee: No problem. What time do you want _____ (start)?
                                                              7

Mary: How about 3:00?

spicy **Sun-Hee:** Great! I'll see you then!

C. COMPOSE Complete the sentences with information about food. Use a verb + infinitive or gerund from the box in each sentence. Share your ideas with a partner.

avoid	buy	drink	feel	go	have	make
bake	cook	eat	find	grow	listen	tell

1. I want _to grow a garden at home_____.

2. I need _____.

3. I try _____.

4. I like _____.

5. I love _____.

6. I hate _____.

iQ PRACTICE   Go online for more practice with verbs + gerunds or infinitives. *Practice › Unit 3 › Activities 9–10*

UNIT ASSIGNMENT
OBJECTIVE ▶

Design a survey and interview a classmate

In this assignment, you are going to design a survey and interview a classmate about his or her food choices. Think about the Unit Question, "How do you choose your food?" Use the listening, the unit video, and your work in this unit. Look at the Self-Assessment checklist on page 56.

CONSIDER THE IDEAS

IDENTIFY Listen to the interview. Match the questions with the student's answers.

1. What's your favorite food? ____

2. Do you think organic food is good for you? ____

3. Why do you avoid strawberries? ____

4. What do you usually eat for breakfast? ____

5. Why do you have that? ____

a. Because I'm allergic to them.

b. Nonfat yogurt with fruit and nuts.

c. I don't know.

d. I think it's healthy.

e. Pizza.

PREPARE AND SPEAK

A. FIND IDEAS Work with a partner. Write ten interview questions.

- Write questions about food likes, dislikes, choices, and opinions.

- Include questions with gerunds and infinitives.

NOTE-TAKING SKILL **Taking notes on an interview**

Before you interview someone, write your interview questions on a piece of paper. Leave room below each question for notes about the speaker's answers. Don't write complete sentences for the answers. Write only the most important words.

Read this sample from an interview.

> Q: What are your favorite foods?
>
> A: Well, I like pizza a lot. I also really like teriyaki chicken. Cherries are my favorite fruit.
>
> Q: What foods do you eat every day?
>
> A: Let's see. I eat yogurt every morning for breakfast. I also have rice with my dinner every day. Sometimes I have rice at lunchtime, too.

Look at the sample notes below. Notice the note-taker left room for notes about the speaker's answers and wrote only the most important words.

Q:	What are your favorite foods?
A:	pizza, teriyaki chicken, cherries
Q:	What foods do you eat every day?
A:	yogurt, rice

B. ORGANIZE IDEAS Work with your partner and prepare your survey.

1. Look at your ten questions from Activity A. Circle your four best questions. Include at least one opinion question.

2. Write your questions. Leave room for notes about the speaker's answers.

iQ PRACTICE Go online for more practice with taking notes on an interview.
Practice > Unit 3 > Activity 11

When you are answering an interviewer's questions, remember to use the phrases *In my opinion* and *I think that* to give your opinion and then give a reason. Review the Speaking Skill box in Unit 2 on page 35 and the Critical Thinking Strategy on page 36.

TIP FOR SUCCESS

When you want more information, you can ask a **follow-up question**. For example: *Why is it your favorite? Why not?*

C. SPEAK Follow these steps. Look at the Self-Assessment checklist below before you begin.

1. Each partner works individually. Use the questions to interview another student in your class. Take notes on his or her answers.

2. Look over your notes. Are they clear? Make changes and add words to make your notes clearer.

3. Work with your partner. Check your notes. Did you write the student's answers correctly?

4. Compare your answers with your partner's answers. How are the answers the same or different? Share your ideas with the class.

iQ PRACTICE Go online for your alternate Unit Assignment.
Practice > Unit 3 > Activity 12

CHECK AND REFLECT

A. CHECK Think about the Unit Assignment as you complete the Self-Assessment checklist.

SELF-ASSESSMENT	Yes	No
Our interview questions were clear.	☐	☐
I used vocabulary from this unit.	☐	☐
I used gerunds and infinitives correctly.	☐	☐
I gave reasons for my opinions when answering questions.	☐	☐

B. REFLECT Discuss these questions with a partner or group.

1. What is something new you learned in this unit?

2. Think about the Unit Question—How do you choose your food? Is your answer different now than when you started this unit? If yes, how is it different? Why?

iQ PRACTICE Go to the online discussion board to discuss these questions.
Practice > Unit 3 > Activity 13

TRACK YOUR SUCCESS

iQ PRACTICE Go online to check the words and phrases you have learned in this unit. *Practice > Unit 3 > Activity 14*

Check (✓) the skills you learned. If you need more work on a skill, refer to the page(s) in parentheses.

LISTENING	☐ I can listen for reasons. (p. 44)
CRITICAL THINKING	☐ I can understand causes and effects. (p. 46)
VOCABULARY	☐ I can use prefixes and suffixes. (p. 48)
PRONUNCIATION	☐ I can recognize stressed syllables. (p. 49)
GRAMMAR	☐ I can use verbs + gerunds or infinitives correctly. (p. 52)
NOTE-TAKING	☐ I can take notes during an interview. (p. 55)
SPEAKING	☐ I can give an opinion. (p. 56)
OBJECTIVE ▶	☐ I can use information and ideas to design a survey and interview a classmate.

4

Sociology

What do you enjoy doing?

A. Discuss these questions with your classmates.

1. Complete the chart. Then compare charts with a partner.

What is . . .	
a fun activity?	
a boring activity?	
an exciting activity?	
a dangerous activity?	
an interesting activity?	

2. Look at the photo. Describe what the person is doing. Why do people do this?

B. Listen to *The Q Classroom* online. Then answer these questions.

1. What did the students say? What are some things they like to do?

2. Do you like the same things that they like?

iQ PRACTICE Go to the online discussion board to discuss the Unit Question with your classmates. *Practice > Unit 4 > Activity 1*

UNIT OBJECTIVE

Listen to a classroom discussion. Use information and ideas to have a group discussion about fun places in your area.

Remember: In conversations, speakers give reasons to explain their activities. They often ask for reasons with **why**. They use words like **because** and **because of** to show they are giving a reason. After *because*, use a complete sentence. After *because of*, use a noun or noun phrase.

A: **Why** do you go to the mall?
B: I go to the mall **because** <u>there are a lot of great shops</u>!
   I go to the mall **because of** <u>the great shops</u>!

Use a T-chart to take notes about activities and reasons. The T-chart below shows an activity and a reason for the example sentences above. A T-chart can help you organize your ideas.

Activity	Reason
go to the mall	a lot of great shops

ANALYZE Listen to two students talking in a shopping mall. Then complete the T-chart below with reasons.

Activity	Reasons
the man comes to the mall	1. to buy clothes 2. _____ 3. _____ 4. _____
the woman comes to the mall	5. _____ 6. _____

iQ PRACTICE Go online for more practice with taking notes on reasons.
Practice > Unit 4 > Activity 2

LISTENING

OBJECTIVE ▶

Free-Time Activities

You are going to listen to a class discussion about free-time activities. Think about what you enjoy doing.

playing a board game

PREVIEW THE LISTENING

A. VOCABULARY Here are some words from the listening. Read the sentences. Then write each underlined word in the correct sentence below.

a. Anna's new house is very <u>modern</u>. It has all the newest technology.

b. From here, we can see the busy market <u>scene</u> below.

c. Picking apples in the fall is a family <u>tradition</u>.

d. In the summer, we sometimes eat <u>outdoors</u>. It's nice to be outside.

e. The tall trees <u>provide</u> shade in the park.

f. Sun-Hee likes to be in <u>nature</u>. She loves trees and flowers.

g. James doesn't like <u>crowded</u> places. There are too many people!

h. Keith likes to read on the weekend. It's very <u>relaxing</u>.

1. I like to sit by the lake in the evening. It's _____.

2. I don't like _____ cars. I like older cars.

3. There are a lot of people here! It's really _____.

4. Some companies _____ free meals for their workers.

5. I love to spend time in _____. I like to look at the trees, the grass, and the animals.

6. The police came to the _____ of the accident.

7. I like to play basketball _____. I don't like to play in a gym.

8. In some countries, it is a _____ to eat special foods on New Year's Day.

iQ PRACTICE Go online for more practice with the vocabulary.
Practice > Unit 4 > Activities 3–4

B. PREVIEW You are going to listen to a discussion about board games and other free-time activities. What do you think the speakers will say about board games? Check (✓) your ideas.

☐ 1. Board games are fun.

☐ 2. People are buying more games.

☐ 3. It can be stressful to play board games when people want to win too much.

☐ 4. People used to play board games, but they don't anymore.

☐ 5. Playing games is relaxing.

☐ 6. Board games are boring.

WORK WITH THE LISTENING

A. CATEGORIZE Read the sentences. Then listen to the discussion. Write *T* (true), *F* (false), or *N* (not enough information).

iQ RESOURCES Go online to download extra vocabulary support.
Resources > Extra Vocabulary > Unit 4

____ 1. The discussion is mostly about video games.

____ 2. All of the speakers are students.

____ 3. The discussion is part of a sociology class.

____ 4. All the speakers have a good opinion of board games.

____ 5. The speakers discuss opinions but not facts.

B. IDENTIFY Listen again. Circle the correct answer.

1. The group are talking about free-time activities you can only do ____.

   a. on weekends

   b. with your friends and family

   c. without a computer or phone

2. Miyumi says that when her brothers are not on their computers, they usually spend time ____.

   a. with their family   b. by themselves   c. outdoors in nature

3. Abdel says that sometimes his friends and family ____.

   a. are too competitive   b. don't care about games   c. like to relax together

4. Miyumi says that free-time activities have different kinds of effects. The effects can depend on ____.

   a. the activity you do   b. the person   c. the time of day

5. Hector says that he ____.

   a. doesn't like board games   b. enjoys walking outdoors   c. always likes being with people

6. Christine says that spending time ____ is very important in today's modern world.

   a. in nature   b. in the city   c. on your computer

SKILL REVIEW Listening for reasons

Remember: In conversations, speakers often use **why** to ask for reasons. They use **because** to give reasons. Review the Listening Skill box in Unit 3 on page 44.

 C. ANALYZE Listen again. Take notes in the chart.

Activity	Reasons
Sales of board games have been going up.	People like to get together [1]_____.
Christine plays board games.	She likes to [2]_____.
Gia plays board games.	It's [3]_____ and _____. They make her [4]_____.
Abdel thinks board games are stressful.	Sometimes people want to [5]_____.
Hector likes to spend time alone.	He thinks it can be [6]_____.

iQ PRACTICE Go online for additional listening and comprehension.
Practice › Unit 4 › Activity 5

CRITICAL THINKING STRATEGY

Noticing differences

When you hear information about more than one thing or person, some information may be different. Listen for words that show differences. Words like *but*, *while*, and *however* introduce differences. Antonyms can also show differences.

Information	Differences
Uma likes to go to museums, **but** Kayla doesn't like museums at all.	Uma and Kayla are different in the way they feel about museums. (Uma's feelings ≠ Kayla's feelings)
Ben thinks lectures are **interesting**. He thinks sports are **boring**.	For Ben, lectures are interesting and sports are boring. *Interesting* and *boring* are antonyms. (Ben's opinion of lectures ≠ Ben's opinion of sports)

iQ PRACTICE   Go online to watch the Critical Thinking Video and check your comprehension. *Practice > Unit 4 > Activity 6*

D. APPLY Listen again. Complete the sentences about differences.

1. _____ thinks board games are _____, but Abdel thinks they are _____.

2. _____ and _____ like to spend time with friends and family, but _____ likes to spend time alone.

3. Gia likes games, but _____ gets mad if she doesn't win.

4. Walking in _____ is less stressful than walking _____.

walking in a park

walking on crowded city streets

E. CREATE Reread sentences 1–3 in Activity D. What are *your* opinions and preferences? Rewrite the sentences with your own information to express differences between you and the people in the listening.

I think board games are fun, but Abdel thinks they are stressful.

1. _____

_____

2. _____

_____

3. _____

_____

F. DISCUSS Work with a partner. Look at Preview the Listening Activity B on page 62. Which statements express ideas that are very different or almost opposite in meaning?

BUILDING VOCABULARY Collocations with *do*, *play*, and *go*

Words for activities often follow the verbs *do*, *play*, and *go*.

They **do gymnastics** on Saturdays.
She **plays basketball** at her school.
He **goes skiing** in the mountains.

do	play	go*
do aerobics	play baseball	go hiking
do crosswords	play Scrabble	go jogging
do gymnastics	play soccer	go shopping
do judo	play tennis	go skiing
do nothing	play video games	go swimming

*You usually use the verb *go* with a gerund (verb + *-ing*).

TIP FOR SUCCESS

The word *let's* introduces suggestions.

A. APPLY Complete the conversations with *play*, *do*, or *go*.

1. **Sara:** Emma, I'm bored. Let's do something.

   Emma: Sure. Let's _____ shopping.

   Sara: I don't like shopping. Let's _____ video games.

   Emma: No, I'm not good at video games. Uh, do you want to _____ hiking?

   Sara: OK. That's a great idea!

2. **John:** Mike, I want to lose weight. What do you do for exercise?

Mike: I _____ judo. I have a class twice a week.

John: Do you still _____ gymnastics?

Mike: No, it was too difficult.

judo

skiing

3. **Sandra:** Mei, do you want to _____ swimming with me?

Mei: No, thanks. I have training.

Sandra: Oh, do you _____ a sport?

Mei: Yes, I _____ soccer. Hey, do you want to _____ skiing this weekend?

Sandra: Sure, that sounds like fun!

B. CREATE Answer the questions with information about yourself. Use *play, do,* or *go.* Then ask and answer the questions with a partner.

1. A: What do you like to do on weekends?

   B: I like to _____.

2. A: What do you like to do at night?

   B: I like to _____.

3. A: What else do you like to do for fun?

   B: I like to _____.

4. A: What do you hate to do?

   B: I really hate to _____.

iQ PRACTICE Go online for more practice with collocations with *do, play,* and *go.*
Practice > Unit 4 > Activity 7

WORK WITH THE VIDEO

A. PREVIEW Do you enjoy making art? Why? Why not?

VIDEO VOCABULARY

artist (n.) a person who makes art, like paintings

clay (n.) a type of sticky dirt that you can use to make bricks or pots

creativity (n.) the use of imagination or new ideas to make something

tile (n.) a thin square of clay or metal

decorate (v.) to make something more attractive by adding to it

a potter making a pot

iQ RESOURCES Go online to watch the video about a pottery competition.
Resources > Video > Unit 4 > Unit Video

B. IDENTIFY Watch the video two or three times. Circle the correct answer.

1. The artists are working on ____.

   a. pots   b. tiles   c. paintings

2. They need to decorate ____ of them.

   a. nine   b. ninety   c. ninety-nine

3. Some artists think their neighbors' ideas might be ____.

   a. the same   b. better   c. worse

4. Some artists are excited because there are many different ____.

   a. competitions   b. winners   c. patterns

5. The ____ look at the artists' work.

   a. judges   b. potters   c. neighbors

6. One way the artists do NOT show creativity is with ____.

   a. the difficulty   b. unusual ideas   c. the order they use

C. EXTEND Would you like to be in a competition like this? Why or why not?

SAY WHAT YOU THINK

A. IDENTIFY Think about the listening and the unit video. Give your opinion about fun. Circle *Yes* or *No* for each sentence. Then compare ideas with a partner.

WHAT MAKES SOMETHING FUN?

1.	Fun activities teach you something.	Yes	No
2.	Fun activities are always active.	Yes	No
3.	Dangerous activities are sometimes fun.	Yes	No
4.	Relaxing activities are not fun.	Yes	No
5.	You need to be with other people to have fun.	Yes	No
6.	It's fun to spend time in nature.	Yes	No
7.	Making something is fun.	Yes	No
8.	It's fun to win.	Yes	No

B. DISCUSS Discuss the questions.

1. What is your favorite activity? Why is it your favorite?

2. Where do you go to do things you enjoy?

SPEAKING

OBJECTIVE ▶ At the end of this unit, you are going to have a group discussion about things you enjoy doing in your area.

GRAMMAR Subject and object pronouns

1. Subjects and objects can be nouns.
   - Subjects come before verbs in statements.
   - Objects come after verbs or prepositions like *at*, *in*, and *on*.

subject	verb	object	preposition + object
Kate	likes	the **book.**	
My **brother**	runs	—	in the **park.**

2. Pronouns replace nouns.
   - You use some pronouns for subjects.
   - You use other pronouns for objects.

	subject pronoun	object pronoun
singular	**I** have a great soccer coach.	He helps **me.**
	You are good at swimming.	I want to go with **you.**
	He goes hiking a lot.	I sometimes see **him** in the park.
	She is good at math.	I like studying with **her.**
	I like the park. **It's** really big.	My friends like **it**, too.
plural	**We** go shopping on Sundays.	Our friends meet **us** at the mall.
	You play baseball a lot.	I sometimes see **you** at the field.
	They are great soccer players.	I like to watch **them.**

3. You usually use the pronouns *he / him, she / her, it / it, we / us*, and *they / them* after you know the noun.

Mary has a brother named Tom. **She** studies with **him** every Friday.

(Mary = **She**; Tom = **him**)

iQ RESOURCES Go online to watch the Grammar Skill Video.
Resources > Video > Unit 4 > Grammar Skill Video

A. IDENTIFY Circle the correct pronoun.

1. (He / Him) goes hiking on Saturdays.

2. Let's go to the mall with (they / them) tomorrow.

3. (We / Us) like to spend time at the park.

4. Sarah's friends make (she / her) laugh.

5. I like this art. (He / It) is beautiful.

6. John and (I / me) love to play tennis.

7. James plays baseball with Sam and (I / me).

8. Fun activities sometimes teach (we / us) something.

B. APPLY Complete each sentence with a pronoun for the underlined word.

1. That TV <u>show</u> is really exciting. I watch _____ every week.

2. Isabel's <u>sister</u> loves to go hiking. _____ goes every weekend.

3. Family <u>traditions</u> are important. I really appreciate _____.

4. I see my <u>grandmother</u> on Wednesdays. I have lunch with _____.

5. My <u>classes</u> are very interesting, but _____ are difficult.

6. <u>Faisal and Miteb</u> go jogging in the park. Then _____ have lunch.

7. <u>We</u> play basketball in the gym. Sometimes our friends join _____.

8. I want to play tennis with <u>you</u>. _____ are an excellent player.

jogging in the park

C. ANALYZE Look back at Activities A and B. Write an *S* over all the subject pronouns. Write an *O* over all the object pronouns.

D. APPLY Complete the conversation with the correct subject and object pronouns.

Sarah: Maria, how do _____ like your cooking class?
1

Maria: I love _____! My teacher is great. She's from France,
2

and _____ really knows how to cook. What's new with you?
3

Sarah: I'm taking a writing class.

Maria: Oh, do _____ write stories?
4

Sarah: No, _____ write poetry. The class is really fun.
5

I like the other students. _____ are very talented.
6

Maria: That's great. Hey, my friends and I are going to the beach this weekend.

Do _____ want to come with _____?
      7   8

Sarah: Sure, that sounds fun and relaxing.

iQ PRACTICE Go online for more practice with subject and object pronouns.
Practice > Unit 4 > Activity 8

iQ PRACTICE Go online for the Grammar Expansion: possessive adjectives.
Practice > Unit 4 > Activity 9

PRONUNCIATION Reduced pronouns

You usually say pronouns quickly, with no stress. When you say *he, him, her,* and *them,* you don't usually pronounce the beginning sounds. You **"reduce"** the words.

| I think **he's** at the park. | I don't see **him.** |
| Is that **her** bike? | Let's call **them.** |

You <u>do</u> pronounce the "h" of *he* when it's the first word in a sentence.

He's at the park.

A. APPLY Complete the conversations with *he, him, her,* and *them.* Then listen and check your answers. Practice the conversations with a partner. Say the reduced forms.

1. A: John is a fun guy. How do you know _____? Does _____ play soccer with you?

   B: No. I know _____ from school. How do you know _____?

   A: _____ spends time at the park near my house. Sometimes _____ plays basketball there with my friends and me.

2. A: Anna's sister Emma is here this weekend. Do you know _____?

   B: Yes, I do. I really like _____.

   A: Me too. Do you think Anna and Emma want to go for a walk with us this afternoon?

   B: Maybe. Let's call _____.

B. COMPOSE Write four sentences with *he, him, her,* and *them.* Then take turns reading your sentences with a partner.

iQ PRACTICE Go online for more practice with reduced pronouns.
Practice > Unit 4 > Activity 10

Use these expressions to **agree** with another person's opinion.

Agreeing with a positive opinion	Agreeing with a negative opinion
A: I like swimming.	A: I don't like swimming.
B: **I do too. / Me too.***	B: **I don't either. / Me neither.***

* *Me too* and *Me neither* sound more informal.

Use these expressions to **disagree** with another person's opinion.
These expressions sound more friendly or polite.

Disagreeing politely	
A: I think that the building is pretty.	A: I love that park. How about you?
B: **Oh, I don't know.**	B: **I'm not sure.**

I do too.

I'm not sure.

A. IDENTIFY Listen to the short conversations. Check (✓) *Agree* or *Disagree* for each conversation. Then listen again and write the expression that you hear.

	Agree	Disagree	Expression
1.	☐	☐	
2.	☐	☐	
3.	☐	☐	
4.	☐	☐	
5.	☐	☐	
6.	☐	☐	

B. CREATE Write six sentences about things that you like or don't like. Then read them to a partner. Your partner will agree or disagree.

1. I really like _____.

2. I don't like _____.

3. I think _____.

4. I think _____.

5. I enjoy _____.

6. I hate _____.

iQ PRACTICE Go online for more practice with agreeing and disagreeing.
Practice > Unit 4 > Activity 11

UNIT ASSIGNMENT
OBJECTIVE ▶

Have a group discussion about things you enjoy doing in your area

In this assignment, you are going to have a group discussion about the "top five" enjoyable things to do in your area. Think about the unit question, "What do you enjoy doing?" Use the listening, the unit video, and your work in this unit. Look at the Self-Assessment checklist on page 74.

CONSIDER THE IDEAS

A. IDENTIFY Listen to a group discuss activities and places they enjoy in their area. What activities do they talk about? Check (✓) the activities. Then compare with a partner.

☐ hiking   ☐ reading books   ☐ taking dance classes

☐ playing tennis   ☐ going to plays   ☐ taking computer classes

☐ playing soccer   ☐ going to a museum   ☐ lying on the beach

☐ going to the gym   ☐ going to concerts   ☐ playing video games

B. EXTEND Do you agree with the answers in Activity A? Do you enjoy those activities? Which activities do you enjoy? Discuss your answers with a partner.

PREPARE AND SPEAK

A. FIND IDEAS What are your five favorite things to do in your area? Complete the chart with your ideas. Give reasons for each place.

Name of activity	Where do you do it?	Why do you enjoy it?
1.		
2.		
3.		
4.		
5.		

B. ORGANIZE IDEAS Choose three ideas from Activity A. Practice different ways to share your ideas. You can use these phrases.

I think that hiking is enjoyable because it's good exercise and it's outdoors.

How about hiking? It lets you get out in nature.

C. SPEAK Work with a group. Discuss your ideas. Look at the Self-Assessment checklist below before you begin.

- Share your three activities and your reasons.

- Listen carefully to others' ideas. Agree or disagree with them.

- As a group, choose the best five activities.

iQ PRACTICE Go online for your alternate Unit Assignment.
Practice > Unit 4 > Activity 12

CHECK AND REFLECT

A. CHECK Think about the Unit Assignment as you complete the Self-Assessment checklist.

SELF-ASSESSMENT	Yes	No
My information was clear.	☐	☐
I used vocabulary from this unit.	☐	☐
I made notes using a T-chart.	☐	☐
I used subject and object pronouns correctly.	☐	☐
I used expressions for agreeing and disagreeing.	☐	☐
I used reduced words correctly.	☐	☐

B. REFLECT Discuss these questions with a partner or group.

1. What is something new you learned in this unit?

2. Think about the Unit Question—What do you enjoy doing? Is your answer different now than when you started this unit? If yes, how is it different? Why?

iQ PRACTICE Go to the online discussion board to discuss these questions.
Practice > Unit 4 > Activity 13

TRACK YOUR SUCCESS

iQ PRACTICE Go online to check the words and phrases you have learned in this unit. *Practice > Unit 4 > Activity 14*

Check (✓) the skills you learned. If you need more work on a skill, refer to the page(s) in parentheses.

NOTE-TAKING	☐ I can take notes on reasons. (p. 60)
LISTENING	☐ I can listen for reasons. (p. 63)
CRITICAL THINKING	☐ I can notice differences. (p. 64)
VOCABULARY	☐ I can understand collocations with *do, play*, and *go*. (p. 65)
GRAMMAR	☐ I can use subject and object pronouns correctly. (p. 69)
PRONUNCIATION	☐ I can reduce the pronouns *he, him, her*, and *them*. (p. 71)
SPEAKING	☐ I can agree and disagree. (p. 72)

OBJECTIVE ▶ ☐ I can use information and ideas to have a group discussion about fun places in my area.

Architecture

UNIT QUESTION

What makes a good home?

A. Discuss these questions with your classmates.

1. Which words are places to live? Circle them. Add two more places.

apartment	house	park
dormitory	mansion	restaurant
garage	office	studio
hotel	_____	_____

2. Use two adjectives to describe your home.

3. Look at the photo. Describe the place. Do you think this is a good place to live? Why or why not?

B. Listen to *The Q Classroom* online. Match the ideas with the students. Then answer the questions.

1. Yuna _____   a. A good home is quiet.

2. Felix _____   b. I want to be right next to the beach!

3. Marcus _____   c. My roommates are nice.

4. Sophy _____   d. Location is important.

5. What are some good things about living with roommates? About living alone?

6. When you choose a home, is location important to you? What else is important?

iQ PRACTICE Go to the online discussion board to discuss the Unit Question with your classmates. *Practice > Unit 5 > Activity 1*

UNIT OBJECTIVE

Listen to a conversation and a town meeting. Use information and ideas to design your perfect home.

LISTENING 1   Let's Find a New Apartment

OBJECTIVE ▶

You are going to listen to a conversation about finding an apartment. Think about what makes a good home.

PREVIEW THE LISTENING

A. VOCABULARY Here are some words from Listening 1. Read the definitions. Then read the sentences. Which explanation is correct? Circle *a* or *b*.

> **comfortable** *(adjective)* 🔑 making you feel physically relaxed
>
> **location** *(noun)* 🔑 OPAL a place where something is or happens
>
> **noisy** *(adjective)* 🔑 making a lot of loud, unpleasant sounds
>
> **private** *(adjective)* 🔑 OPAL for one person or group only, and not for everyone else
>
> **problem** *(noun)* 🔑 OPAL a thing that is difficult to deal with or understand
>
> **public transportation** *(noun phrase)* the system of buses, trains, etc., that run according to a schedule and that anyone can use
>
> **rent** *(noun)* 🔑 the money that you regularly pay to live in a house, an apartment, etc.
>
> **roommate** *(noun)* a person that you share a room with, especially at a college or university

🔑 Oxford 3000™ words   **OPAL** Oxford Phrasal Academic Lexicon

1. Rob watches loud TV shows. His apartment is <u>noisy</u>.

   a. Rob's apartment is quiet.

   b. Rob's apartment isn't quiet.

2. Marta likes her <u>private</u> room, but she sometimes gets lonely.

   a. Marta doesn't share her room with anyone.

   b. Marta shares her room with someone.

ACADEMIC LANGUAGE

The corpus shows that *location* is more common in academic writing than in academic speaking.

_____| OPAL
Oxford Phrasal Academic Lexicon

3. Matt's apartment is in a great <u>location</u>. It's on a quiet street near his school.

   a. His apartment is cheap and very large.

   b. His apartment is in a convenient place.

4. Sara has a <u>comfortable</u> chair. She likes to sit in it.

   a. The chair is very soft.

   b. The chair is very hard.

5. David's <u>rent</u> is really expensive, so he wants to get a roommate.

   a. David's apartment is free.

   b. David pays a lot of money for his apartment.

6. Jamal and Saud are <u>roommates</u>. They both live in Room 215.

   a. Jamal and Saud live together.

   b. Jamal and Saud have a class together.

7. There's a big <u>problem</u> with this apartment. It doesn't have a kitchen!

   a. The apartment is a good choice.

   b. The apartment is not a good choice.

8. Our city doesn't have <u>public transportation</u>. People usually walk or drive.

   a. The city has no streets or sidewalks.

   b. The city has no buses or trains.

iQ PRACTICE Go online for more practice with the vocabulary.
Practice > Unit 5 > Activities 2–3

B. PREVIEW Karen and Lisa are looking for a new apartment. You are going to listen to them tell their friend Atifa about the apartments that they looked at today. Think about the perfect apartment. What are two things you want and two things you don't want?

I want: a big kitchen   I don't want: noisy neighbors

I want: _____ _____

I don't want: _____ _____

WORK WITH THE LISTENING

🔊 **A. INVESTIGATE** Listen to the conversation. On a separate piece of paper, take notes on each of the three apartments: one on First Street, one next to the beach, and one downtown. Use the example below to guide you.

iQ RESOURCES Go online to download extra vocabulary support.
Resources > Extra Vocabulary > Unit 5

On First Street	Next to the beach	Downtown
great location	beautiful building	2 bedrooms

B. IDENTIFY Look at your notes. Write the correct apartment below each picture: *First Street*, *Beach*, or *Downtown*.

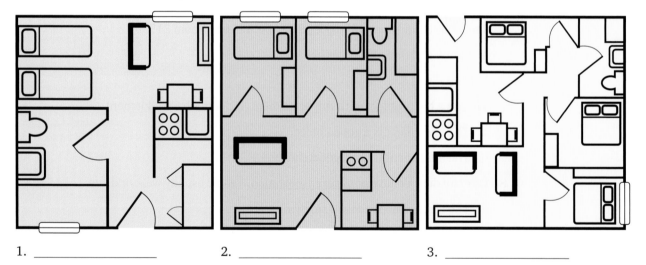

1. _____   2. _____   3. _____

C. CATEGORIZE Look at these statements. Which are good points and which are bad points? Write each statement in the correct part of the chart on page 81.

The rent is expensive.	It's noisy.
The neighbors seem nice.	It's far from campus.
The rent is cheap.	It doesn't have private bedrooms.
It's close to a lot of restaurants and shops.	It's near public transportation.
It's close to campus.	The bathroom is very small.

	First Street	Beach	Downtown
Good points			
1. _____	☐	☐	☐
2. _____	☐	☐	☐
3. _____	☐	☐	☐
4. _____	☐	☐	☐
5. _____	☐	☐	☐
Bad points			
1. _____	☐	☐	☐
2. _____	☐	☐	☐
3. _____	☐	☐	☐
4. _____	☐	☐	☐
5. _____	☐	☐	☐

🔊 **D. IDENTIFY** Listen again. Check (✓) the correct apartment for each point in the chart. You will check some items more than once.

🔊 **E. CATEGORIZE** Listen again. Read the statements. Write *T* (true) or *F* (false). Then correct the false statements.

_____ 1. The apartment on First Street is Lisa's favorite.

_____ 2. Karen's favorite is the apartment downtown.

_____ 3. The apartment near the beach is in a nice building.

_____ 4. The apartment downtown has big bedrooms.

_____ 5. The apartment on First Street has three bedrooms and two bathrooms.

_____ 6. The apartment near the beach isn't very private.

_____ 7. The apartment downtown is across the street from school.

F. EVALUATE Which apartment do you like: the one on First Street, the one near the beach, or the one downtown? Why?

I like _____ because . . .

iQ PRACTICE Go online for additional listening and comprehension. *Practice > Unit 5 > Activity 4*

 CRITICAL THINKING STRATEGY

Ranking information

When you **rank** items or information in a list, you number them in a particular order, for example, order of importance.

If you are ranking a lot of information, you can break the list into parts, for example: important, less important, and not important. Then rank the items in each part.

iQ PRACTICE Go online to watch the Critical Thinking Video and check your comprehension. *Practice > Unit 5 > Activity 5*

G. ANALYZE Read the sentences. What is important to you? Check (✓) five sentences. Then rank them from 1 to 5. (Put a *1* next to the most important thing.)

What Do You Want in a Home?

○ ____ I want to live in a convenient location, near stores and restaurants.

○ ____ I don't want to pay a lot of rent.

○ ____ I want a private room.

○ ____ I want to live with my extended family.

○ ____ I want to live with good friends.

○ ____ I want to have nice neighbors.

○ ____ I want a home near public transportation.

○ ____ I want to live near a garden or park.

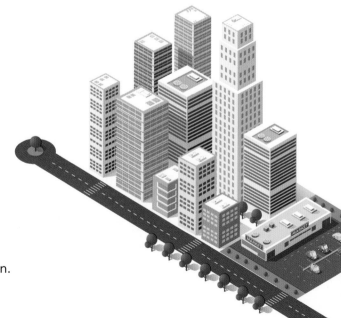

? SAY WHAT YOU THINK

A. EVALUATE Work with a partner. Compare your answers in Activity G on page 82. Do you and your partner agree or disagree?

B. EXPLAIN With your partner, discuss the reasons for your answers to Activity G. Do you want to change any of your answers?

LISTENING SKILL Listening for opinions

Remember: An opinion is something that a person thinks or feels. Speakers sometimes use *I think (that)* when they give an opinion.

🔊 ⬜ **I think that** this house is very beautiful.   **I think** the location is very good.

Sometimes speakers give opinions with the words they choose. Listen for verbs (*like, love,* and *hate*), adjectives (*cheap, expensive, beautiful,* and *ugly*), or the word *only*.

⎡ **I love** this apartment.   It's **expensive**.
⎣ The rent is **only** $400 a month. (= I think that the rent is low.)

---

iQ RESOURCES Go online to watch the Listening Skill Video.
Resources > Video > Unit 5 > Listening Skill Video

🔊 **IDENTIFY** Listen to the conversations. What opinions do you hear? Check (✓) them.

1. Rob and Sam look at an apartment.

   ⬜ Rob and Sam like the location.

   ⬜ They think the apartment is too far from school.

   ⬜ They think that the rent is expensive.

   ⬜ They think the rent is good.

2. Mary talks to her mother.

   ⬜ Mary likes taking the bus.

   ⬜ Mary doesn't like taking the bus.

   ⬜ Mary likes her neighbors.

   ⬜ Mary doesn't like her neighbors.

3. Matt visits James's new house.

   ⬜ Matt likes James's new house.

   ⬜ Matt doesn't like James's new house.

   ⬜ James thinks that there are a lot of bedrooms.

   ⬜ James thinks that there aren't a lot of bedrooms.

4. Kate gets a new apartment.

☐ Kate likes the living room in her new apartment.

☐ Kate doesn't like the living room in her new apartment.

☐ Mika thinks the apartment is in a good location.

☐ Mika thinks the apartment is in a bad location.

iQ PRACTICE Go online for more practice with listening for opinions. *Practice > Unit 5 > Activity 6*

NOTE-TAKING SKILL **Taking notes on pros and cons**

When you are listening to people talk about the pros (good things) and cons (bad things) about a topic, you can use a T-chart to take notes. Remember to write only the important words in your notes.

Read part of the conversation from Listening 1.

> Lisa: I think the apartment on First Street was my favorite. It's in a great location, and it's really big.
>
> Karen: That's true. It's across the street from school. The rent is expensive, though.
>
> Lisa: Yeah, but it has three big bedrooms. We can get another roommate.
>
> Karen: Hmm, maybe. But the bathroom is really small.

Look at the notes below. Notice the note-taker wrote the pros on one side of the chart and the cons on the other side.

Pros	Cons
great location	expensive rent
big	small bathroom
three big bedrooms	

INVESTIGATE Listen to a conversation between John and Amanda. Complete the T-chart with the pros and cons for John's home.

Pros	Cons

iQ PRACTICE Go online for more practice with taking notes on pros and cons. *Practice > Unit 5 > Activity 7*

Housing Problems, Housing Solutions

OBJECTIVE ▶   You are going to listen to a town meeting about building housing for students. Think about what makes a good home.

PREVIEW THE LISTENING

A. VOCABULARY Here are some words from Listening 2. Read the definitions. Then complete the sentences below.

> **affordable** *(adjective)* not expensive
>
> **condition** *(noun)* 🔑 OPAL something in good condition is not damaged or broken
>
> **demand** *(noun)* 🔑 OPAL a need or want
>
> **entertainment** *(noun)* 🔑 fun or free-time activities
>
> **housing** *(noun)* 🔑 apartments, houses, and homes
>
> **increase** *(verb)* 🔑 OPAL to become bigger
>
> **landlord** *(noun)* a person—he or she rents homes to people for money
>
> **shortage** *(noun)* not enough of something

🔑 Oxford 3000™ words   **OPAL** Oxford Phrasal Academic Lexicon

VOCABULARY SKILL REVIEW

In Unit 4, you learned about collocations with *do*, *play*, and *go*. Look at the sentences in Activity A. Can you find any collocations with *play*?

1. This house is in bad _____. There are holes in the walls, and it has two broken windows.

2. I have to talk to my _____. The lock on my front door is broken. I want him to fix it.

3. This apartment isn't _____. It's just too expensive!

4. We are having a water _____. People need to save water.

5. _____ in this area is a big problem. There aren't enough apartments or houses.

6. Rents _____ every year. I have to pay 2 percent more this year.

7. There is a big _____ for dormitory rooms this year. Everyone wants to live in the dorms.

8. Video games are my favorite type of _____. I try to play video games every weekend.

iQ PRACTICE   Go online for more practice with the vocabulary.
Practice > Unit 5 > Activities 8–9

B. PREVIEW You are going to listen to Dr. Ross Chan. He is at a town meeting. He wants the city of Jackson to build more housing for students. Read the sentences below. Check (✓) the possible problems.

☐ There are not many dormitories.

☐ Many apartments aren't affordable for students.

☐ Some cheap apartments are near entertainment, like restaurants.

☐ Some apartments are near the campus and in safe areas.

☐ Rents are not increasing.

☐ Some inexpensive housing is in bad condition.

WORK WITH THE LISTENING

A. IDENTIFY Listen to Dr. Chan. He mentions three housing choices for students. What are they? Circle the correct numbers.

iQ RESOURCES   Go online to download extra vocabulary support.
Resources > Extra Vocabulary > Unit 5

1. Students can live in cheap apartments downtown.

2. They can live with many friends in a house.

3. They can live in cheap hotel rooms.

4. They can go to a different university.

5. They can live at home with their families.

B. CATEGORIZE Write your answers from Activity A on the lines. Then listen again. Write the pros and cons for each housing choice in the T-chart.

Housing choice 1: _____

Pros	Cons

Housing choice 2: _____

Pros	Cons

Housing choice 3: _____

Pros	Cons

C. EVALUATE Look at the pros and cons in your T-charts in Activity B on page 87. Which housing choice do you think is the best? Why? Write three reasons. Then discuss your answer with a partner.

Best choice: _____

Reason 1: _____

Reason 2: _____

Reason 3: _____

D. CATEGORIZE Read the statements. Listen again. Write *T* (true) or *F* (false). Then correct the false statements.

_____ 1. The new campus is large.

_____ 2. There are a lot of fun things to do downtown.

_____ 3. The apartments downtown are not in good condition.

_____ 4. More people want to live downtown.

_____ 5. The neighborhoods near campus are safe.

_____ 6. All students can live with their families.

_____ 7. The new university can increase business in Jackson.

_____ 8. The city doesn't want the university to grow.

the city of Jackson

WORK WITH THE VIDEO

A. PREVIEW What are three important things to have in a very small house? Discuss with a partner.

Jack Sparrow House, Cornwall, UK

iQ RESOURCES Go online to watch the video about a very small house.
Resources › Video › Unit 5 › Unit Video

B. IDENTIFY Watch the video two or three times. Then match the sentence halves to make true statements.

1. Theo and Bee make videos about ____
2. There are a lot of shelves in ____
3. Bee and Theo disagree about the size of ____
4. Bee's favorite part of the house is ____
5. Theo's favorite part of the house is ____
6. The house is near ____

a. the sofa.
b. the garden.
c. the kitchen.
d. the ocean.
e. things they like.
f. the bedroom.

C. EXTEND Would you like to live in this house? Why or why not?

SAY WHAT YOU THINK

SYNTHESIZE Think about Listening 1, Listening 2, and the unit video as you discuss the questions.

1. What are three important things to have in a home?

2. What are three possible problems with a home?

3. Do you think the small house in the video would be a good solution for Lisa and Karen in Listening 1? How about the city of Jackson? Explain.

BUILDING VOCABULARY Compound nouns

Compound nouns are two-word nouns. The first noun is like an adjective. It describes the second noun. You write some compound nouns as one word and some as two words.

One word: bathtub, streetcar, backyard
Two words: shopping mall, police officer, public transportation

A. IDENTIFY Read the sentences. Circle the compound nouns.

1. He parks his car in the driveway, not in the garage.

2. The apartment has three bedrooms and two bathrooms.

3. There is a swimming pool in the backyard.

4. They like to sit by the fireplace and read.

5. She doesn't have a mailbox, so she gets her mail from the post office.

6. I need to buy a smoke alarm for the living room.

7. There is a drugstore near my home.

8. There is a bookshelf in the dining room.

He parks in the driveway.

B. APPLY Read the definitions. Then write a compound noun from the Building Vocabulary box or from Activity A.

TIP FOR SUCCESS

To make a plural compound noun, add an -s to the end of the compound noun. Don't add an -s to the first word in the noun.
Correct: *post offices*
Incorrect: *posts offices*

1. _____ People get their mail from this place.

2. _____ People put their books on this.

3. _____ You can park your car here.

4. _____ You burn wood in it for heat.

5. _____ This is an open area behind a house.

6. _____ You buy medicine here.

7. _____ You can buy clothes, books, and other items here.

8. _____ This is a kind of transportation in a city.

90 UNIT 5 What makes a good home?

iQ PRACTICE Go online for more practice with compound nouns.
Practice > Unit 5 > Activity 10

PRONUNCIATION Stress in compound nouns

In compound nouns, the stress is usually on the **first** word of the compound.

☐ **post** office   **book**shelf   **drug**store

A. IDENTIFY Listen to the compound nouns. The speaker will say each compound noun twice. Which pronunciation is correct? Circle *a* or *b*.

1. swimming pool   a   b   6. post office   a   b

2. bookshelf   a   b   7. grandson   a   b

3. bedroom   a   b   8. mailbox   a   b

4. shopping mall   a   b   9. living room   a   b

5. driveway   a   b   10. fireplace   a   b

swimming pool   fireplace

B. COMPOSE Write six sentences with compound nouns from Activity A. Then read your sentences to a partner.

1. _____

2. _____

3. _____

4. _____

5. _____

6. _____

iQ PRACTICE Go online for more practice with stress in compound nouns.
Practice > Unit 5 > Activity 11

SPEAKING

OBJECTIVE ▶   At the end of this unit, you are going to design your perfect home and present your design to the class.

GRAMMAR *Part 1* Prepositions of location

Prepositions of location answer the question "Where?"

Use *in* with countries and cities.

◻ The Eiffel Tower is **in Paris.**

Use *on* with the names of streets and roads.

◻ The apartment is **on Oak Street.**

Use *at* with a place in a city or a specific address.

◻ The study group meets **at my house.**   My house is **at 333 Oak Street.**

A. APPLY Circle the correct preposition.

1. Sam is staying (in / on / at) his brother's apartment.

2. Emma lives (in / on / at) Shanghai.

3. Hassan's house is (in / on / at) Oak Street.

4. The post office is (in / on / at) 415 First Street.

5. The bank is (in / on / at) Ocean Avenue.

6. The university is (in / on / at) Miami.

B. CREATE Answer the questions with information about you. Use *in*, *on*, and *at* in your answers. Practice the questions and answers with a partner.

1. A: What country do you live in?

    B: _____.

2. A: What city do you live in?

    B: _____.

3. A: What street do you live on?

    B: _____.

4. A: What address do you live at?

    B: _____.

5. A: Where do you like to study?

    B: _____.

Look at the map and read the paragraph. Notice the bold prepositions of location.

> The bank is **next to** the library. The library is **between** the bank and the gift shop. The gift shop is **across** (the street) **from** the bookstore. The bookstore is **on the corner of** Oak Street and Central Avenue. The parking lot is **behind** the supermarket.

C. APPLY Look at the map. Complete the sentences with prepositions of location.

1. The library is _____ the bank.

2. The gift shop is _____ Oak Street and Central Avenue.

3. The playground is _____ Jackson Park.

4. The movie theater is _____ the bookstore and the coffee shop.

5. The coffee shop is _____ the supermarket.

6. Jackson Park is _____ Oak Street and Central Avenue.

7. The bookstore is _____ the movie theater.

8. The bank is _____ Jackson Park.

D. ANALYZE There is an error in each sentence. Find the errors and correct them.

1. My apartment building is ~~on~~ *at* 698 Pine Street.

2. The bookstore is in the corner of Central Avenue and Oak Street.

3. The library is between to the bank and the gift shop.

4. The gift shop is across the street to Jackson Park.

5. The parking lot is behind of the supermarket.

6. The movie theater is next from the coffee shop.

E. CREATE Write sentences about places in your city. Use the prepositions of location.

1. (on the corner of) _____

   _____

2. (across the street from) _____

   _____

3. (behind) _____

   _____

4. (between) _____

   _____

5. (next to) _____

   _____

iQ PRACTICE   Go online for more practice with prepositions of location.
Practice › Unit 5 › Activities 12–13

Design a home and give a presentation

In this assignment, you are going to design your perfect home and present your design to the class. Think about the unit question, "What makes a good home?" Use Listening 1, Listening 2, the unit video, and your work in this unit. Look at the Self-Assessment checklist on page 96.

CONSIDER THE IDEAS

IDENTIFY Listen to the presentation. Check (✓) the ideas that the speakers give.

1. What is the inside of the house like?	
☐ four bedrooms	☐ comfortable chairs and sofas
☐ three bathrooms	☐ a big television
☐ a big kitchen	☐ big windows
☐ a big living room	

2. What is the outside of the home like?	
☐ a big backyard	☐ trees and flowers
☐ a big front yard	☐ a big driveway
☐ a table with chairs	☐ a swimming pool

3. What is the neighborhood like?	
☐ near a shopping mall	☐ near a supermarket
☐ across the street from a park	☐ quiet
☐ near public transportation	☐ nice neighbors

PREPARE AND SPEAK

A. FIND IDEAS Work in a group of three. Make a chart like the one above. Talk about the questions in the chart and write down your ideas. During your discussion, name pros and cons of living in different places. Use expressions for giving your opinions, agreeing, and disagreeing.

SKILL REVIEW Agreeing and disagreeing

Remember: During your discussion, you can agree and disagree politely using the expressions below. Review the Speaking Skill box in Unit 4 on page 72.

Agreeing	I do too. / Me too.	I don't either. / Me neither.
Disagreeing	Oh, I don't know.	I'm not sure.

B. ORGANIZE IDEAS Look at your chart in Activity A. Choose the four most important items for each question. Follow these steps.

1. Draw a map of your perfect home.

   • Draw the rooms inside the house.

   • Draw the outside of the house.

   • You can also show some of the neighborhood.

2. Each person chooses one part of the home to describe.

3. Practice your presentation.

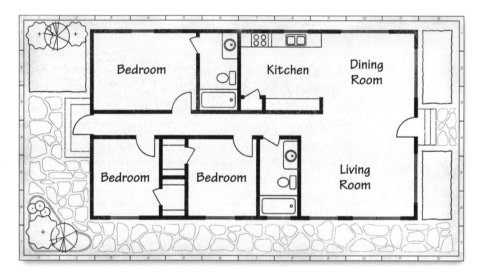

C. SPEAK Put your home drawing on the wall. Take turns presenting information about your home. Look at the Self-Assessment checklist below before you begin.

iQ PRACTICE Go online for your alternate Unit Assignment.
Practice > Unit 5 > Activity 14

CHECK AND REFLECT

A. CHECK Think about the Unit Assignment as you complete the Self-Assessment checklist.

SELF-ASSESSMENT	Yes	No
My information was clear.	☐	☐
I used vocabulary from this unit.	☐	☐
I used prepositions of location correctly.	☐	☐
I listened for the opinions of my group members.	☐	☐
I agreed and disagreed with opinions appropriately.	☐	☐

B. REFLECT Discuss these questions with a partner or group.

1. What is something new you learned in this unit?

2. Think about the Unit Question—What makes a good home? Is your answer different now than when you started this unit? If yes, how is it different? Why?

iQ PRACTICE Go to the online discussion board to discuss these questions. *Practice > Unit 5 > Activity 15*

TRACK YOUR SUCCESS

iQ PRACTICE Go online to check the words and phrases you have learned in this unit. *Practice > Unit 5 > Activity 16*

Check (✓) the skills you learned. If you need more work on a skill, refer to the page(s) in parentheses.

CRITICAL THINKING	☐ I can rank information in order of importance. (p. 82)
LISTENING	☐ I can identify opinions. (p. 83)
NOTE-TAKING	☐ I can take notes on pros and cons. (p. 84)
VOCABULARY	☐ I can use compound nouns. (p. 90)
PRONUNCIATION	☐ I can pronounce compound nouns correctly. (p. 91)
GRAMMAR	☐ I can use prepositions of location. (pp. 92, 93)
SPEAKING	☐ I can agree and disagree. (p. 95)

OBJECTIVE ▶ ☐ I can use information and ideas to design a home and give a presentation.

6 Health Sciences

What do you do to stay healthy?

A. Discuss these questions with your classmates.

1. Check (✓) the statements that are true for you. Then compare with a partner. How do you think these things affect your health?

   ☐ I eat a lot of sweets.   ☐ I watch television every day.

   ☐ I exercise a lot.   ☐ I am on a sports team.

   ☐ I drink a lot of water.   ☐ I worry a lot.

2. Look at the photo. How do these people stay healthy? Do you enjoy this activity? Why or why not?

B. Listen to *The Q Classroom* online. Then answer these questions.

1. What did the students say? Who do you think has the healthiest habits?

2. Which student are you most like? How?

iQ PRACTICE   Go to the online discussion board to discuss the Unit Question with your classmates. *Practice > Unit 6 > Activity 1*

UNIT OBJECTIVE Listen to two podcasts. Use information and ideas to make a health survey and discuss it with a partner.

LISTENING 1

Health Watch

OBJECTIVE ▶

You are going to listen to a podcast about stress. Think about how you stay healthy.

PREVIEW THE LISTENING

A. VOCABULARY Here are some words from Listening 1. Read the definitions. Then complete the sentences below.

ACADEMIC LANGUAGE

We often use the word *stress* with these verbs: *manage* stress, *reduce* stress, *control* stress, *create* stress, and *cause* stress.

──────────┘ OPAL
Oxford Phrasal Academic Lexicon

diet *(noun)* 🔑 the food that you usually eat

energy *(noun)* 🔑 OPAL the ability to be very active or do a lot of work without getting tired

lonely *(adjective)* 🔑 sad because you are not with other people

manage *(verb)* 🔑 to control something

reduce *(verb)* 🔑 OPAL to make something smaller

run-down *(adjective)* very tired and not healthy, often because you are working too hard

stress *(noun)* 🔑 OPAL a feeling of being very worried because of problems in your life

🔑 Oxford 3000™ words   OPAL Oxford Phrasal Academic Lexicon

1. Ziyad is sad because he feels _____. He doesn't have many friends in his new city.

In Unit 3, you learned about prefixes and suffixes. Look at the sentences in Activity A. Can you find any words with the prefix *un*-? A form of the word *stress* is *stressful*. What do you think the suffix *-ful* means?

2. Kate works 60 hours a week. She wants to _____ her time at work to 40 hours a week.

3. Lin is feeling a lot of _____ right now. She has three exams this week!

4. I don't have any _____. I feel tired all the time.

5. Sam has an unhealthy _____. He has pizza and soda for lunch every day. He hardly ever eats vegetables.

6. Anna doesn't _____ her schedule very well. She's always late, and she often forgets to do her homework.

7. Hiroshi is working two jobs and taking four classes. He looks really

_____.

iQ PRACTICE Go online for more practice with the vocabulary.
Practice > Unit 6 > Activities 2–3

B. PREVIEW You are going to listen to an interview with Dr. Michael Smith about stress. When do you think people feel stress? Check (✓) your answers and add one more idea.

People can feel stress when . . .

☐ they have money problems.   ☐ they have healthy diets.

☐ they want good grades.   ☐ they are lonely.

☐ they work long hours.   ☐ _____

WORK WITH THE LISTENING

A. IDENTIFY Listen to the podcast. Circle the correct answer.

iQ RESOURCES Go online to download extra vocabulary support.
Resources > Extra Vocabulary > Unit 6

1. What is the weekly podcast about?

   a. exercise   c. health

   b. money   d. students

2. What is a big cause of stress these days?

   a. People are very busy.   c. People don't have jobs.

   b. People eat bad food.   d. People are lonely.

3. What are two causes of stress for many students?

   a. money and health   c. diet and no exercise

   b. work and grades   d. grades and children

4. What is "a great way to reduce stress"?

   a. getting a job   c. having children

   b. exercising every day   d. laughing

B. IDENTIFY Listen again. What ideas and topics does the interview mention? Circle them.

vacations	money	sickness	exercise	coffee
work	rent	headaches	food	friends
children	grades	sleep	vegetables	medicine

C. CATEGORIZE Read the sentences in the chart. Then listen again. Check (✓) the correct column for each sentence.

TIP FOR SUCCESS

The verb *cause* means "to make something happen." Here, you see the noun form of *cause*. It means "a thing that makes something happen."

	Causes of stress	Symptoms of stress	Ways to reduce stress
1. People feel run-down.	☐	✓	☐
2. They exercise.	☐	☐	☐
3. They worry about money.	☐	☐	☐
4. They have a good diet.	☐	☐	☐
5. They're very busy.	☐	☐	☐
6. They don't have energy.	☐	☐	☐
7. They feel lonely.	☐	☐	☐
8. They have social time.	☐	☐	☐
9. They gain weight.	☐	☐	☐
10. They worry about grades.	☐	☐	☐

D. CATEGORIZE Read the sentences. Write *T* (true) or *F* (false). Then correct the false statements.

_____ 1. People are too busy because they feel stress.

_____

_____ 2. Many people have children and work full-time.

_____

____ 3. Dr. Smith thinks that money is sometimes a cause of stress.

_____

____ 4. Students don't often have problems with stress.

_____

____ 5. Some people have stress because of worrying.

_____

____ 6. Stress sometimes makes people sick.

_____

____ 7. Exercise does not reduce stress.

_____

____ 8. Laughter helps reduce stress.

_____

iQ PRACTICE Go online for additional listening and comprehension.
Practice > Unit 6 > Activity 4

SAY WHAT YOU THINK

EXTEND When do you feel stress? Add one idea to the chart. Check (✓) your answers. Then discuss your answers with a partner.

	A lot of stress	A little stress	Not any stress
With my family	☐	☐	☐
At school	☐	☐	☐
With my neighbors	☐	☐	☐
At work	☐	☐	☐
With my friends	☐	☐	☐
_____	☐	☐	☐

Frequency means "How often?" When you listen, try to hear these frequency adverbs and expressions.

Adverbs of frequency	always, usually, often, sometimes, hardly ever, never
Expressions with *every*	**every** day, **every** week, **every** year
Other expressions	**once a** week, **twice a** month, three **times a** year eight **hours a** day, four **hours a** week

A: Do you **always** exercise at the gym?
B: No, **sometimes** I jog in the park.
A: How often do you exercise?
B: **Three times a week**.

A. IDENTIFY Listen to eight parts of a conversation. Circle the words and expressions you hear. (Three items have two answers.)

1. always	sometimes	every week
2. never	every day	once a week
3. twice a week	never	sometimes
4. six days a week	twice a week	every day
5. always	sometimes	three times a week
6. once a week	usually	twice a week
7. usually	once a day	always
8. every week	once a day	three times a week

B. IDENTIFY Read the questions. Listen to the whole conversation. Circle the correct answer.

1. How many days a week does John work?

   a. five   b. six   c. seven

2. How often does John exercise?

   a. every day   b. twice a week   c. never

3. How often does Anna go to the gym?

   a. three times a week   b. twice a week   c. every day

4. How often does Anna go running?

   a. twice a week   b. three times a week   c. once a week

5. How often does John drink coffee with his meals?

   a. sometimes   b. always   c. usually

C. INVESTIGATE Ask and answer these questions with a partner. Write your partner's answers.

HEALTH QUESTIONNAIRE

1. How many times a week do you exercise?

_____

2. How often do you eat fast food?

_____

3. How often do you eat vegetables?

_____

4. How often do you drink coffee or soda?

_____

5. How many hours a week do you work?

_____

6. How many days a week do you go to school?

_____

iQ PRACTICE Go online for more practice with listening for frequency.
Practice > Unit 6 > Activity 5

In Unit 4 on page 60, you learned about using a T-chart. When you listen, sometimes you hear a lot of information. For example, two or three people talk about their lives. For complicated information, a T-chart is too simple. Use a bigger chart. Look at the chart below. The more complicated information about each person is clearly organized.

Name	Healthy Habits	Unhealthy Habits
Jin	eats a lot of vegetables	doesn't work out at all
Tania	takes supplements	eats a lot of junk food

 CATEGORIZE Listen to three students talk about their healthy and unhealthy habits. Then complete the chart with the missing information.

Name	Healthy habits	Unhealthy habits
Emma	works out five days a week	
Amal		
John		

iQ PRACTICE Go online for more practice with taking notes in a chart. *Practice › Unit 6 › Activity 6*

LISTENING 2 Vitamin Supplements

OBJECTIVE ▶

You are going to listen to a podcast about health habits and vitamin supplements. Think about how you stay healthy.

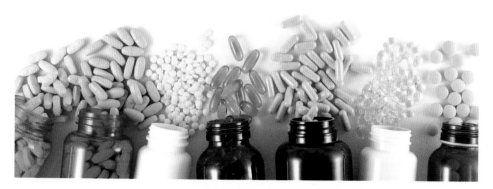

PREVIEW THE LISTENING

A. VOCABULARY Here are some words from Listening 2. Read the definitions. Then read the sentences. Which explanation is correct? Circle *a* or *b*.

> **control** *(noun)* 🔑 OPAL the power or ability to decide what happens
>
> **depends on** *(verb phrase)* 🔑 OPAL isn't certain
>
> **exercise** *(verb)* 🔑 OPAL to move your body to keep it strong and well
>
> **healthy** *(adjective)* 🔑 well; not often sick
>
> **pill** *(noun)* a small, often round, hard piece of medicine that you swallow
>
> **produce** *(verb)* 🔑 OPAL to make or grow something
>
> **vitamin** *(noun)* 🔑 one of the things in food that you need to be healthy

🔑 Oxford 3000™ words   **OPAL** Oxford Phrasal Academic Lexicon

1. It's important to have <u>control</u> of what you eat so you can be healthy. You can do this by cooking your own meals.

   a. It's important to be able to decide what you eat.

   b. It's important to eat food that tastes good.

2. If you want to be <u>healthy</u>, eat a lot of fruit and vegetables and don't have a lot of candy and soda.

   a. Being healthy is good.   b. Being healthy isn't good.

3. I <u>exercise</u> five days a week. I usually go jogging, but sometimes I go to the gym.

   a. Exercising isn't good for your body.   b. Exercising is good for your body.

4. Fatima's company <u>produces</u> exercise clothes.

   a. Fatima's company makes exercise clothes.

   b. Fatima's company buys exercise clothes.

5. Carrots have <u>vitamins</u> that are good for your eyes and bones.

   a. Eating carrots can cause problems with your eyes and bones.

   b. Carrots have things in them that make you healthy.

6. How much food should Hassan eat every day? It <u>depends on</u> how much he exercises.

   a. The speaker is sure how much food Hassan should eat every day.

   b. The speaker is not sure how much food Hassan should eat every day.

7. I took a <u>pill</u> for my headache. I feel better now.

   a. The speaker had some medicine.   b. The speaker slept for a little while.

iQ PRACTICE Go online for more practice with the vocabulary.
Practice › Unit 6 › Activities 7–8

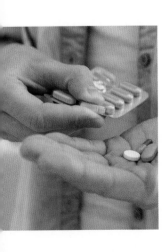

B. PREVIEW You are going to listen to an interview with a nutrition expert about health habits and vitamin supplements. Write answers to the questions. Then compare answers with a partner.

1. Do you think people take vitamin supplements more or less now than they did in the past?

   _____

2. Why do you think people take vitamins?

   _____

3. Do you think everyone should take vitamins? Why or why not?

   _____

   _____

WORK WITH THE LISTENING

A. IDENTIFY Listen to the podcast about health habits and vitamin supplements. Check (✓) the correct person for each description.

iQ RESOURCES Go online to download extra vocabulary support.
Resources > Extra Vocabulary > Unit 6

	Tran	Gina
1. never takes vitamin supplements	☐	☐
2. takes vitamin supplements every day	☐	☐
3. always eats good food	☐	☐
4. doesn't eat well	☐	☐
5. exercises every day	☐	☐
6. exercises twice a week	☐	☐

B. IDENTIFY Listen again and complete the sentences. You will not use two of the words and phrases in the box.

better	eat	health	not need
diet	exercise	more	worse

1. If you have a balanced _____, you may _____ supplements.

2. People are taking _____ supplements than before because they want to have control of their _____.

3. Supplements make people feel _____ about themselves when they don't _____ well.

C. ANALYZE Listen again. Each of these statements is false. Correct them to make true statements.

1. A balanced diet doesn't include fruits and vegetables.

   _____

2. A balanced diet includes whole-grain cereals and beef.

   _____

3. Tran eats oily fish once a week.

   _____

4. Next year, people will probably spend less money on supplements.

   _____

5. About 60 percent of Americans take supplements.

   _____

6. American manufacturers make 30–40 billion dollars' worth of supplements every month.

   _____

   _____

D. ANALYZE Read about the people at the gym. According to Tran, should they take supplements or not?

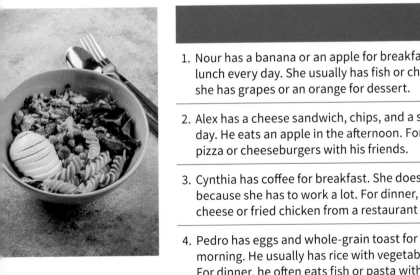

	Supplements: yes or no?
1. Nour has a banana or an apple for breakfast and a salad for lunch every day. She usually has fish or chicken for dinner, and she has grapes or an orange for dessert.	
2. Alex has a cheese sandwich, chips, and a soda for lunch every day. He eats an apple in the afternoon. For dinner, he usually has pizza or cheeseburgers with his friends.	
3. Cynthia has coffee for breakfast. She doesn't have time for lunch because she has to work a lot. For dinner, she has pasta with cheese or fried chicken from a restaurant near her house.	
4. Pedro has eggs and whole-grain toast for breakfast every morning. He usually has rice with vegetables for lunch. For dinner, he often eats fish or pasta with vegetables.	

CRITICAL THINKING STRATEGY

Relating to ideas

To **relate** to an idea is to connect yourself to it. Relating to an idea helps you understand it better. When you learn about a new idea, think about your opinions about it or how it might affect you.

iQ PRACTICE Go online to watch the Critical Thinking Video and check your comprehension. *Practice > Unit 6 > Activity 9*

E. CATEGORIZE Read the meal descriptions in Activity D again. How are they similar to or different from your diet? Take notes in the chart. Then rank the diets from 1 (most similar to yours) to 4 (least similar to yours). Share with a partner.

Others' diets	Similarities to my diet	Differences from my diet	Ranking
1. Nour			
2. Alex			
3. Cynthia			
4. Pedro			

F. CREATE Write answers to the questions.

1. What do you usually eat for breakfast, lunch, and dinner?

_____

_____

_____

_____

2. Do you think you have a balanced diet? Explain.

_____

_____

3. Based on your answers to questions 1 and 2, do you think you should take supplements? Why or why not?

_____

_____

WORK WITH THE VIDEO

A. PREVIEW What do you know about yoga? Discuss with a partner.

iQ RESOURCES Go online to watch the video about Sarita, a dancer and yoga teacher. *Resources > Video > Unit 6 > Unit Video*

B. IDENTIFY Watch the video two or three times. Then match the sentence halves to make true statements.

1. Sarita is ____
2. She teaches ____
3. She does ____
4. She doesn't do ____
5. She sells ____
6. After work, she goes to ____
7. Her favorite part of yoga class is ____
8. After she teaches yoga, she ____
9. When she has free time, she ____
10. Dancing and teaching yoga make her ____

a. ballet.
b. yoga in her free time.
c. the yoga school.
d. tired, but happy and healthy.
e. a professional dancer.
f. the end.
g. modern dance.
h. a dance DVD.
i. goes home and makes dinner.
j. socializes with friends.

C. EXTEND Do you want a daily schedule like Sarita's? Why or why not?

SAY WHAT YOU THINK

A. CREATE Make true statements about your health habits. Circle your answers and add your own idea. Then check (✓) your good habits.

Good Habits

1. I (exercise / don't exercise) regularly. ☐
2. I (eat / don't eat) fresh fruit and vegetables. ☐
3. I (eat / don't eat) a lot of junk food. ☐
4. I (sleep / don't sleep) at least eight hours a night. ☐
5. I (work / don't work) too much. ☐
6. I (watch / don't watch) what I eat. ☐
7. I (do / don't do) relaxing activities. ☐
8. Your idea: _____ ☐

B. SYNTHESIZE Think about Listening 1, Listening 2, and the unit video as you discuss the questions.

1. What are your healthy habits?
2. What are your unhealthy habits?
3. How well do you manage stress?

BUILDING VOCABULARY Adjectives ending in -ed

Many adjectives end with -ed. These adjectives come from verbs. They usually describe a feeling or an emotion.

Verbs	John <u>worries</u> a lot.	Anna likes to <u>relax</u> at the park.
Adjectives	John is **worried**.	Anna is **relaxed**.

Adjectives ending in -ed look like past tense verbs. A verb usually comes after a noun or subject pronoun. (*Anna **surprised** us.*) An adjective usually comes after a form of *be*. (*Anna is **surprised**.*)

Here are some other adjectives ending with -ed.

☐ bored   confused   excited   interested   tired

A. APPLY Read the sentences. Complete each sentence with the adjective form of the word in bold.

1. Mary **worries** about school. She is always _____.
2. Running doesn't **interest** me. I'm not _____ in running.

3. Soccer games **excite** James. He is _____ about playing soccer today.

4. Sam **relaxes** on the weekends. On Saturdays, he is usually _____.

5. These questions **confuse** me. I'm _____.

B. APPLY Complete each conversation with a word from the box. Then practice the conversations with a partner. You won't use all the words.

bored   excited   interested   relaxed   surprised   tired   worried

1. A: What's wrong?

   B: Oh, I'm a little _____. I stayed awake really late last night.

2. A: I'm _____. Let's do something fun.

   B: Do you want to play tennis?

3. A: Guess what! My brother wants to go to the gym with us tomorrow!

   B: Wow, I'm _____! He hates exercising!

4. A: I'm _____ about the final exam. This class is really difficult for me.

   B: I plan to study with Isabel and Emma tonight. You can join us.
      Are you _____?

   A: Yes, I am! Thanks!

iQ PRACTICE Go online for more practice with adjectives ending in *-ed*.
Practice > Unit 6 > Activity 10

SPEAKING

OBJECTIVE ▶

At the end of this unit, you are going to make a health survey and discuss it with a partner.

GRAMMAR Modals *can* and *should*

1. A modal comes before a base form verb. Modals can be affirmative or negative.*

   I **should eat** more fruit.
   ‾‾‾‾‾ ‾‾‾
   modal   base verb

   I **can't sleep** some nights.
   ‾‾‾‾ ‾‾‾‾‾
   modal   base verb

   Don't put an *-s* at the end of the verb.

   ✓ Correct: He **can play** tennis well.   ✗ Incorrect: He **can plays** tennis well.

2. Use *can / can't* to talk about possibility or ability.

   Stress **can make** people gain weight.   Rob **can't swim**.

3. Use *should / shouldn't* to give advice.

   You **should exercise** every day.   You **shouldn't worry** all the time.

   *The full forms of *shouldn't* and *can't* are *should not* and *cannot*.

iQ RESOURCES   Go online to watch the Grammar Skill Video.
Resources > Video > Unit 6 > Grammar Skill Video

He works too much.

A. APPLY Complete the conversation with *can, can't, should,* and *shouldn't*. Then practice with a partner.

Hyo: I'm worried about Martin. He looks really tired. He works too much.

Jamal: I know. He _____ work so much.
                            1

Hyo: You're right. He _____ sleep more, too. He sleeps about four hours
                                 2
a night! And he doesn't exercise.

Jamal: He _____ come to the gym with me. There's a swimming pool there.
                      3

Hyo: Well, he _____ swim, but he wants to learn. Does your gym have
                          4
swimming lessons?

Jamal: Yes, it does. He _____ take lessons in the evenings or on the
                                    5
weekends.

Hyo: Oh, good. You _____ call him and tell him that. I _____
                              6   7
come, too. I need to learn how to swim.

Jamal: Yes, that's a great idea!

B. CREATE Write three sentences about stress in your life and your unhealthy habits. (Look at your answers in the *Say What You Think* activities on pages 103 and 112.)

C. CREATE Take turns reading your sentences with a partner. Give your partner advice. Use *should* and *shouldn't*.

A: I feel a lot of stress because I worry about grades.
B: Hmm. You should . . .

iQ PRACTICE Go online for more practice with the modals *can* and *should*.
Practice > Unit 6 > Activity 11

iQ PRACTICE Go online for the Grammar Expansion: modals *have to* and *has to*. *Practice > Unit 6 > Activity 12*

PRONUNCIATION Stressing important words

Speakers sometimes stress important words, like nouns, verbs, and adverbs of frequency. Speakers use stress to:

- **answer a question.** Speakers stress the words with the answer to the question.

- **correct mistakes.** Speakers stress the word they are correcting.

Answering a question	Correcting a mistake
A: How often do you exercise? B: I exercise **every day**.	A: I can swim. B: You can't swim? A: No, I **can** swim.

A. IDENTIFY Underline the words the speakers stress to correct a mistake. Listen to check your answers. Then practice the conversations with a partner.

1. A: Are you worried?

   B: No, I'm feeling <u>relaxed</u>.

2. A: Do you go to the gym on Fridays?

   B: No, I go on Saturdays.

3. A: Should I drive downtown?

   B: No, you should walk!

4. A: Do you exercise every day?

   B: No, I only exercise on the weekends.

5. A: I can't play tennis.

   B: You can play tennis?

   A: No, I can't play tennis.

fast food

B. CREATE Write answers to the questions. Then circle the stressed words in your answers.

1. How often do you exercise?

_____

2. What do you worry about?

_____

3. How much stress do you have in your life?

_____

4. How often do you eat fast food?

_____

C. DISCUSS Work with a partner. Ask and answer the questions in Activity B.

iQ PRACTICE Go online for more practice with stressing important words. *Practice > Unit 6 > Activity 13*

SPEAKING SKILL Asking for repetition

Use these expressions to ask for repetition when you don't understand something.

Excuse me?	Sorry. What did you say?
A: Do you worry about money?	A: There's a new health-food restaurant downtown.
B: **Excuse me?**	B: **Sorry. What did you say?**
A: Do you sometimes worry about money?	A: There's a new restaurant downtown. They have health food.
B: No, not really.	B: Oh, that sounds good!

We often use the expression *I'm sorry. Could you repeat that?* when we have asked for information but don't understand the answer.

We often ask for repetition of **numbers** because many numbers have similar sounds.

I'm sorry. Could you repeat that?

A: How much does the health club cost?
B: It's $30 a month.
A: **I'm sorry. Could you repeat that?**
B: Sure. It's $30 every month.

A. IDENTIFY Listen to Martin talk to his doctor. Answer the questions.

1. What are Martin's symptoms?

   a. He is always worried and unhappy.   b. He is always tired and often sick.

2. How many hours does he work every week?

   a. 15 or 16   b. 50 or 60

3. How often does Martin take vacations?

   a. once a year   b. never

4. What does he sometimes do for exercise?

   a. He swims.   b. He runs.

B. DISCUSS Work with a partner. Ask and answer these questions about health. Ask for repetition.

1. What do you worry about?

2. How often do you feel tired?

3. How many hours do you work or study?

4. What should you do more of?

5. What are five things that you can do to stay healthy?

iQ PRACTICE Go online for more practice with asking for repetition.
Practice > Unit 6 > Activity 14

UNIT ASSIGNMENT Make and discuss a health survey

OBJECTIVE ▶

In this assignment, you are going to make a health survey. Then you are going to discuss the survey with a partner. Think about the Unit Question, "What do you do to stay healthy?" Use Listening 1, Listening 2, the unit video, and your work in this unit. Look at the Self-Assessment checklist on page 118.

CONSIDER THE IDEAS

IDENTIFY Listen to some students discuss their survey. Check (✓) the questions that you hear.

☐ 1. How many hours do you work every week?

☐ 2. How many hours do you sleep every night?

☐ 3. How often do you exercise?

☐ 4. What do you do with your friends?

☐ 5. What do you do to relax?

PREPARE AND SPEAK

A. FIND IDEAS Work with a partner. Write six questions about health habits. Include questions about diet, sleep, and work.

B. ORGANIZE IDEAS With your partner, look at your health questions from Activity A. Choose the three best questions.

C. SPEAK Follow these steps. Look at the Self-Assessment checklist below before you begin.

1. Work individually. Ask three students your questions. You and your partner should talk to different people.

2. Share your survey answers with your partner. Discuss your survey results.

iQ PRACTICE   Go online for your alternate Unit Assignment.
Practice > Unit 6 > Activity 15

CHECK AND REFLECT

A. CHECK Think about the Unit Assignment as you complete the Self-Assessment checklist.

SELF-ASSESSMENT	Yes	No
My information was clear.	☐	☐
I used vocabulary from this unit.	☐	☐
I used a chart to take notes.	☐	☐
I used the modals *can, can't, should,* and *shouldn't* correctly.	☐	☐
I used adjectives ending in *-ed* correctly.	☐	☐
I listened for frequency words and expressions.	☐	☐

B. REFLECT Discuss these questions with a partner or group.

1. What is something new you learned in this unit?

2. Think about the Unit Question—What do you do to stay healthy? Is your answer different now than when you started this unit? If yes, how is it different? Why?

iQ PRACTICE   Go to the online discussion board to discuss these questions.
Practice > Unit 6 > Activity 16

TRACK YOUR SUCCESS

iQ PRACTICE Go online to check the words and phrases you have learned in this unit. *Practice* > *Unit 6* > *Activity 17*

Check (✓) the skills you learned. If you need more work on a skill, refer to the page(s) in parentheses.

LISTENING	☐ I can identify frequency words and expressions. (p. 104)
NOTE-TAKING	☐ I can use a chart to take notes. (p. 106)
CRITICAL THINKING	☐ I can relate to ideas I hear. (p. 110)
VOCABULARY	☐ I can understand some adjectives ending in -ed. (p. 112)
GRAMMAR	☐ I can use the modals can and should. (p. 114)
PRONUNCIATION	☐ I can stress important words in a sentence. (p. 115)
SPEAKING	☐ I can ask for repetition. (p. 116)

OBJECTIVE ▶ ☐ I can use information and ideas to make a health survey and discuss it with a partner.

Global Studies

7

Where do you want to travel?

A. Discuss these questions with your classmates.

1. What are three places in your city or town that you think visitors would like to see?

2. What activities can you do in your city or town?

3. What is your favorite city? Why?

4. Look at the photo. What do you see? Why do you think people come to this city?

B. Listen to *The Q Classroom* online. Then answer these questions.

1. Where do the students want to travel?

2. Did the students mention places or activities that you listed in Activity A? Which ones?

3. Which do you like better, big cities or small towns?

iQ PRACTICE Go to the online discussion board to discuss the Unit Question with your classmates. *Practice > Unit 7 > Activity 1*

UNIT OBJECTIVE

Listen to a radio program and a conversation. Use information and ideas to give a presentation about where you want to travel.

It's important to take organized notes that show you how ideas are related. An **informal outline** is an easy way to see how one idea is related to another idea. It's also easy to find information in your notes when you study.

Read this sample from a radio show.

> David: Thanks for joining us on *Travel Talk*, Amy. What city did you visit?
>
> Amy: I'm happy to be here, David. I visited Seoul, South Korea, last month. It's a beautiful city with interesting architecture. There are big skyscrapers downtown. And there are some traditional wooden houses, too.

Look at the page of notes. Notice the note-taker used an informal outline. The bigger, more important ideas are close to the left margin of the paper. Details about each big idea are below and to the right.

City
Seoul
Architecture
skyscrapers
traditional wooden houses

APPLY Read the rest of the conversation. Take informal notes on the food and activities in Seoul.

David: Did you like the food?

Amy: The food was great. It was spicy and delicious. I really liked the noodles and the beef.

David: What kinds of things did you do?

Amy: Well, I did a lot of shopping. Seoul has some great department stores. There are also some very nice outdoor markets.

David: That sounds like fun. What else did you do?

Amy: I went hiking one day in the mountains.

iQ PRACTICE Go online for more practice with taking notes in an informal outline. *Practice > Unit 7 > Activity 2*

LISTENING 1

Travel Talk

OBJECTIVE ▶

You are going to listen to a radio program about three special cities. Think about where you want to travel.

PREVIEW THE LISTENING

A. VOCABULARY Here are some words from Listening 1. Read the definitions. Then read the sentences. Which explanation is correct? Circle *a* or *b*.

> **average** *(adjective)* 🔑 OPAL ordinary, not special
>
> **climate** *(noun)* 🔑 OPAL the regular pattern of weather in a place
>
> **culture** *(noun)* 🔑 OPAL the customs, ideas, and way of life of a group of people or a country
>
> **historic** *(adjective)* 🔑 important in history
>
> **lecture** *(noun)* 🔑 OPAL a talk that is given to a group of people to teach them about a particular subject, often as part of a university or college course
>
> **recently** *(adverb)* 🔑 OPAL not long ago
>
> **skyscraper** *(noun)* a very tall building in a city

🔑 Oxford 3000™ words   OPAL Oxford Phrasal Academic Lexicon

1. The <u>climate</u> of Tunisia includes hot and dry summers.

   a. The weather is hot and dry in Tunisia in the summer.

   b. The beaches of Tunisia are hot and dry in the summer.

2. The <u>average</u> tourist stays at this hotel for one week, but Anna really likes it here. She is staying for two weeks.

   a. Anna is like most tourists at the hotel.

   b. Anna is not like most tourists at the hotel.

3. Many tourists visit Paris because it is a center for French <u>culture</u>. They go to Paris to have good French food, visit museums, and see beautiful old buildings.

   a. You can learn a lot about French customs and culture in Paris.

   b. You can do a lot of shopping in Paris.

4. You can walk through the gardens at the park. You can also go to <u>lectures</u> there. You can listen to someone give a talk about a subject you are interested in.

   a. A lecture is a kind of talk.

   b. A garden is a kind of talk.

5. Mary <u>recently</u> visited Shanghai. She was there last month.

   a. Mary visited Shanghai a short time ago.

   b. Mary visited Shanghai a long time ago.

6. Rome has many <u>historic</u> buildings. For example, the famous Roman Forum is about 2,000 years old.

   a. Rome has many important new buildings.

   b. Rome has many important old buildings.

the Roman Forum

7. Rio de Janeiro has a lot of <u>skyscrapers</u>. One of them is Ventura Corporate Towers. It has 36 floors. Some skyscrapers have more than 40 floors.

   a. There are a lot of big offices in Rio.

   b. There are a lot of tall buildings in Rio.

iQ PRACTICE Go online for more practice with the vocabulary.
Practice > Unit 7 > Activities 3–4

B. PREVIEW You are going to listen to a radio program about three special cities. Look at the pictures. Match each description with the correct picture.

1. ____   2. ____   3. ____

a. Ubud is on an island in Bali, in Indonesia.

b. Bruges is a historic city in Belgium. It has canals and colorful houses.

c. New York City is a busy city in the United States.

WORK WITH THE LISTENING

A. IDENTIFY Listen to the radio program. The interviewer talks to three people. Match each person with the correct city.

iQ RESOURCES Go online to download extra vocabulary support. *Resources > Extra Vocabulary > Unit 7*

1. David ____   a. Bruges

2. Amanda ____   b. Ubud

3. Sam ____   c. New York City

4. Mika ____   d. does not name a city

B. IDENTIFY Listen again and complete the outline below.

Amanda
_____

  City: _____

  Architecture
_____

_____

  Food
_____

    delicious

  Activities
_____

Other information

on Bali in Indonesia, warm climate, cool and comfortable forests,

center for culture

Sam

City: _____

Architecture

_____

Food

_____

Activities

museums

Mika

City: _____

Architecture

_____

Food

_____

Activities

shopping, eating at restaurants and cafes

Other information

big, modern, busy, over 8 million people

C. CATEGORIZE Look at the outline in Activity B. Check (✓) the topics that
each speaker talks about.

	climate	architecture	food	shopping	museums	lectures	walks
Amanda							
Sam							
Mika							

D. CATEGORIZE Read the descriptions of the people. Match each person with the best vacation city. Use the information in your notes in Activity B.

a. Ubud   b. Bruges   c. New York

____ 1. Eric likes modern cities. He loves to go to museums. He also loves to go shopping and eat different kinds of food.

____ 2. Theresa loves to go to places with beautiful, warm weather.

____ 3. Jonas likes European cities. He is interested in European history.

____ 4. (describe yourself) _____

_____

____ 5. (describe a friend or family member) _____

_____

iQ PRACTICE Go online for additional listening and comprehension.
Practice > Unit 7 > Activity 5

SKILL REVIEW Listening for frequency

Remember: Frequency means "How often?" When you listen, try to hear frequency adverbs and expressions like *usually* and *every night*. Review the Listening Skill box in Unit 6 on page 104.

E. IDENTIFY Read the sentences. Then listen to the radio program again. Circle the correct answer.

1. The average temperature in Bali is ____.

    a. cool   b. very warm   c. very hot

2. Amanda enjoyed going to lectures and taking walks ____.

    a. every evening   b. every weekend   c. every week

3. Mika visits New York ____.

    a. twice a month   b. twice a year   c. every year

4. On her last visit, Mika ____ every day.

    a. went to museums   b. shopped   c. ate Ethiopian food

iQ PRACTICE Go online for more practice with listening for frequency.
Practice > Unit 7 > Activity 6

SAY WHAT YOU THINK

A. CATEGORIZE Work with a partner. Choose a city that you both know. Complete the chart individually.

City: _____	Not good	OK	Good
1. culture	☐	☐	☐
2. architecture	☐	☐	☐
3. weather	☐	☐	☐
4. shopping	☐	☐	☐
5. food	☐	☐	☐

B. CREATE Discuss your chart with your partner. Give reasons for your answers.

A: *I think the culture in Mexico City is good.*

B: *I agree. You can go to a lot of museums there.*

the Museo Soumaya

Traveling Alone

You are going to listen to three friends talk about traveling alone. Think about where you want to travel.

PREVIEW THE LISTENING

A. VOCABULARY Here are some words from Listening 2. Read the sentences. Then write each underlined word next to the correct definition.

> **ACADEMIC LANGUAGE**
> We often use the word *decision* with the verb *make*: *make a decision*. We also often use an adjective in front of *decision*: ***big** decision*, ***important** decision*, ***difficult** decision*.
>
> ─────────── OPAL
> Oxford Phrasal Academic Lexicon

1. One <u>advantage</u> of taking a vacation with a friend is you always have someone to talk to during your trip.

2. I have to make a <u>decision</u>. Should I go to Peru or Portugal this summer?

3. I'm so <u>disappointed</u>. I can't go to Karen's party tonight because I'm sick. I really wanted to go.

4. Carlos doesn't want to go. Alan doesn't want to go <u>either</u>.

5. I have my suitcase and my passport. What <u>else</u> do I need?

6. I enjoyed my trip to India. It was a fantastic <u>experience</u>.

7. Ivan is <u>nervous</u> about the trip. He doesn't like flying.

8. I don't know what we should do today. Let's do <u>whatever</u> you want to do.

a. _____ something that has happened to you

b. _____ used with *not* to show agreement with a negative statement

c. _____ more; extra

d. _____ anything or everything

e. _____ a choice that you make after thinking

f. _____ feeling sad because what you wanted did not happen

g. _____ something that helps you or that is useful

h. _____ worried or afraid

iQ PRACTICE Go online for more practice with the vocabulary.
Practice › Unit 7 › Activities 7–8

B. PREVIEW You are going to hear Luna, Pia, and Melissa talk about
traveling alone. Look at the photo. How do you think this person feels
about traveling alone? How do you feel about traveling alone? Discuss your
answer.

WORK WITH THE LISTENING

 A. CATEGORIZE Listen to the conversation. Then complete the statements in
the chart with ideas from the listening.

iQ RESOURCES Go online to download extra vocabulary support.
Resources › Extra Vocabulary › Unit 7

Traveling alone	Traveling with friends
1. You talk to _____.	1. You only talk to _____.
2. You can make all the _____.	2. You don't do activities with _____.
3. You can do whatever _____.	3. You do things that _____.

B. IDENTIFY Listen again. Match the sentence halves to make true statements.

1. Luna's sister can't go to Tokyo because she ____

2. Pia can't go to Tokyo because she ____

3. Melissa can't go to Tokyo because she ____

4. Luna feels ____

5. Pia feels ____

6. Melissa talked to ____

7. Pia likes traveling alone because she ____

a. excited about traveling alone.

b. nervous about traveling alone.

c. can do what she wants.

d. a lot of new people on her trip.

e. has to go to school during the summer.

f. doesn't have enough money.

g. has to work during the summer.

CRITICAL THINKING STRATEGY

Inferring

When you **infer** or **make inferences**, you make guesses based on information that you hear. To infer, ask yourself, "What *else* does this information tell me?"

> Pia: I only visited one [museum] because I was in Mexico with some friends. They didn't want to go to museums. They just wanted to go shopping and go to the beach all the time.

This information tells us that Pia was disappointed that she only went to one museum. We can also infer that she didn't really want to go shopping and go to the beach the whole time.

iQ PRACTICE Go online to watch the Critical Thinking Video and check your comprehension. *Practice > Unit 7 > Activity 9*

C. APPLY Work with a partner. Ask what he or she is going to do tonight or this weekend. Try to infer how he or she feels about it. Report back to the class. Your partner will confirm if your inferences are correct.

D. INTERPRET What can you infer from these statements from Listening 2? Circle the correct answer. Some items have more than one answer.

1. **Pia:** "I have to go home and work at my family's restaurant again this summer. I made a lot of money last summer."

   a. Pia's family's restaurant is not near her college.

   b. Pia doesn't like working in her family's restaurant.

   c. Pia worked in her family's restaurant last summer.

2. **Pia:** "I made all the decisions and did whatever I wanted. For example, I went to about ten art museums during my trip."

   a. Pia doesn't enjoy making decisions when she's traveling.

   b. Pia is good at making decisions.

   c. Pia likes art.

3. **Melissa:** "One of them lives in Los Angeles. Now we see each other a couple of times a week."

   a. Melissa probably lives close to Los Angeles.

   b. Melissa's new friend goes to school in Los Angeles.

   c. Melissa enjoys spending time with her new friend.

WORK WITH THE VIDEO

A. PREVIEW Answer the questions.

VIDEO VOCABULARY

village (n.) a very small town

ferry (n.) a boat that takes people or things on short trips across a river or on an ocean

first class (n.) the part of a train, airplane, etc., that is more expensive to travel in

motorboat (n.) a small, fast boat that has a motor

1. What are two reasons why someone might not visit different places in their own country?

   _____

   _____

   _____

   _____

2. What are some benefits of traveling in your own country?

   _____

   _____

iQ RESOURCES   Go online to watch the video about Nadiya's journey.
Resources > Video > Unit 7 > Unit Video

B. IDENTIFY Watch the video two or three times. Then circle the correct answer.

1. Nadiya lives in (the United Kingdom / Bangladesh).

2. When Nadiya arrives in Dhaka, she goes shopping for (spices / food).

3. Nadiya leaves Dhaka on (a train / a ferry).

4. She (has her own room / has to share a room).

5. Nadiya gets on a motorboat. It is her (third time / first time) on a motorboat.

6. Children are using boats to (fish / go to school).

7. Nadiya wants her family to (stay in their village / travel outside of their village).

C. EXTEND What parts of your country have you visited? What did you do there? What parts would you like to visit? Why?

SAY WHAT YOU THINK

SYNTHESIZE Think about Listening 1, Listening 2, and the unit video as you discuss the questions.

1. What are some differences between traveling to a different country and traveling around your own country?

2. What are you more interested in—traveling in your own country or traveling to a different country? Why?

Word families are groups of similar words. Word families can include nouns, verbs, adjectives, and adverbs. For example, look at the related forms of this word:

Verb:	correct
Adjective:	correct
Noun:	correction
Adverb:	correctly

When you look up a word in the dictionary, look for other forms of the word. You can find other word forms in, above, and below the definition. For example, look at the different words forms in and below the definitions of *locate* and *special*.

lo·cate /ˈloʊkeɪt/ *verb* (lo·cates, lo·cat·ing, lo·cat·ed)
to find the exact position of someone or something: *Rescue helicopters are trying to locate the missing sailors.*
▸ lo·cat·ed /ˈloʊkeɪt̬əd/ *adjective*
in a place: *The factory is located near the river.*

lo·ca·tion /loʊˈkeɪʃn/ *noun* [count]
a place: *The house is in a quiet location at the top of a hill.*

spe·cial¹ /ˈspɛʃl/ *adjective*
1 not usual or ordinary; important for a reason: *It's my birthday today, so we're having a special dinner.*
2 for a particular person or thing: *He goes to a special school for deaf children.*
spe·cial·ize /ˈspɛʃlˌaɪz/ *verb* (spe·cial·iz·es, spe·cial·iz·ing, spe·cial·ized)
specialize in something to study or know a lot about one subject, type of product, etc.: *He specialized in criminal law.*
spe·cial·ly /ˈspɛʃl·i/ *adverb*
for a particular purpose or reason: *a specially designed chair*

All dictionary entries adapted from the *Oxford Basic American Dictionary for learners of English* © Oxford University Press 2011.

A. APPLY Circle the correct word form in each sentence. Use the definitions above to help you.

1. This is (special / specially / specialize) food from China. It's sweet.

2. We can't find Khalid. We are trying to (locate / location / located) him.

3. John and Sam are chefs. They (special / specially / specialize) in food from Turkey.

4. Melbourne is in a great (locate / location / located). It's next to the ocean and close to beautiful mountains.

5. My parents cooked me a (special / specially / specialize) meal for my graduation.

6. The museum is (locate / location / located) near city hall.

7. Our lunch is (special / specially / specialize) prepared. The chef cooked it just for us!

B. APPLY Write the part(s) of speech for each word. Then complete the sentences with the words. Use your dictionary to help you.

a. architect _____

b. architecture _____

c. lecturer _____

d. lecture _____

e. recent _____

f. recently _____

g. variety _____

h. various _____

1. Matt designs buildings. He is a(n) _____.

2. I tried _____ restaurants in China, and they were all great.

3. In Cairo, we visited a(n) _____ of monuments.

4. Toshi _____ returned from Tokyo.

5. The _____ from the college gave a very interesting talk on the history of Saudi Arabia.

6. I want to study the _____ in Istanbul. The buildings there are beautiful.

7. Mary is a wonderful public speaker. She wants to _____ at universities.

8. I met Carlos on my _____ trip to Rio.

Matt designs buildings.

Mary enjoys public speaking.

iQ PRACTICE Go online for more practice with using the dictionary.
Practice > Unit 7 > Activity 10

SPEAKING

OBJECTIVE ▶

At the end of this unit, you are going to give a presentation about a place that you want to visit.

GRAMMAR Past of *be*; Simple past affirmative statements

Past of *be*

Use the past of *be* to identify and describe people and things in the past.

Affirmative and negative statements			
subject	*be*	*(not)*	
I	**was**		very happy.
You / We / They	**were**	**(not)**	busy yesterday.
He / She / It	**was**		in Ubud last week.

- You can contract negative statements:

  was not = wasn't   were not = weren't

- Past time expressions answer the question "When?"

  last + time: **last** week, **last** month
  time + **ago**:   three days **ago**, one year **ago**

Yes / No questions			Answers	
be	subject		*yes*	*no*
Was	he	in China?	Yes, he **was**.	No, he **wasn't**.
Were	they	excited?	Yes, they **were**.	No, they **weren't**.

Information questions			Answers
wh- word	*be*	subject	
How	**were**	Paris and Rome?	They **were** great!
What	**was**	your favorite city?	Istanbul **was** my favorite city.
When	**was**	the lecture?	The lecture **was** last week.

Simple past affirmative statements

The simple past describes completed actions in the past.

Regular past verbs end in *-ed*. The simple past form is the same for all subjects.

> I **visited** Brazil last year.
> They **liked** their trip to Tokyo.
> He **shopped** downtown yesterday.
> We **stayed** at a nice hotel.

Spelling simple past verbs

like–lik**ed**	stay–stay**ed**	try–tr**ied**
shop–shop**ped**	travel–travel**ed**	visit–visit**ed**

iQ RESOURCES Go online to watch the Grammar Skill Video.
Resources > Video > Unit 7 > Grammar Skill Video

A. APPLY Put the words in the correct order. Use the correct simple past form of *be* in each question. Then ask and answer the questions with a partner.

1. you / where / yesterday / be ?

   _____

2. last week / be / you / on vacation ?

   _____

3. be / last trip / how / your ?

   _____

4. last vacation / it / be / on / your / cold ?

   _____

5. be / when you were young / what / your favorite city ?

   _____

6. in this city / you / be / last year ?

   _____

7. what / as a child / your favorite food / be ?

   _____

8. your childhood heroes / you / be / who ?

   _____

B. APPLY Complete Sarah's email about her trip to Istanbul. Use the past form of the words in the box.

| shop | stay | travel | try | visit | walk |

To: annatwo@email.org
From: sarahfive@email.org
Subject: My trip to Istanbul

Dear Anna,

I'm back from my vacation! I _____ to Istanbul last month. My trip
                              1
was so much fun! I _____ in a really nice hotel. There was a view of a
                    2
beautiful park outside my window. I _____ a lot of great museums.
                                     3
I also _____ around the city every day. The food was delicious.
        4
I _____ baklava for the first time. It's a dessert made with nuts and
   5
syrup. On my last day, I _____ at a big market. There were so many
                          6
pretty scarves, shoes, and bags. Let's get together soon. I have a gift for you!

See you soon!

Sarah

the Grand Bazaar
in Istanbul

C. CREATE Write about a city you visited. Complete the sentences. Then read your sentences to a partner.

1. I traveled to _____.

2. I visited _____.

3. I tried _____.

4. I loved _____.

5. I stayed _____.

6. There was / were _____.

iQ PRACTICE Go online for more practice with the past of *be* and simple past affirmative statements. *Practice > Unit 7 > Activity 11*

iQ PRACTICE Go online for the Grammar Expansion: past time expressions. *Practice > Unit 7 > Activity 12*

PRONUNCIATION *-ed* endings

There are three ways to pronounce the *-ed* ending of a simple past verb.

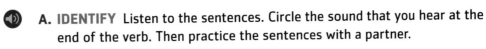

/t/		/d/		/ɪd/	
walk**ed**	lik**ed**	travel**ed**	lov**ed**	visit**ed**	want**ed**

A. IDENTIFY Listen to the sentences. Circle the sound that you hear at the end of the verb. Then practice the sentences with a partner.

1. They collected shells on the beach in Oman. /t/ /d/ /ɪd/
2. We tried to go to the Natural History Museum. /t/ /d/ /ɪd/
3. He shopped all afternoon. /t/ /d/ /ɪd/
4. We started our tour at noon. /t/ /d/ /ɪd/
5. I worked in Dubai last year. /t/ /d/ /ɪd/
6. Heavy traffic caused problems in Los Angeles. /t/ /d/ /ɪd/

They collected shells.

B. CREATE Write four sentences about a special city. Use verbs from the box.

enjoyed	needed	shopped	stayed	visited
liked	relaxed	started	tried	wanted

1. _____
2. _____
3. _____
4. _____

C. IDENTIFY Read your sentences from Activity B to a partner. Circle the sounds you hear in your partner's sentences.

1. /t/ /d/ /ɪd/
2. /t/ /d/ /ɪd/
3. /t/ /d/ /ɪd/
4. /t/ /d/ /ɪd/

iQ PRACTICE Go online for more practice with *-ed* endings.
Practice > Unit 7 > Activity 13

Look at the two conversations below. In Conversation 1, Isabel asks a **closed question** (a *yes/no* question), and Sun-Hee answers "Yes." In Conversation 2, Isabel asks an **open question** (a *wh-* question). Sun-Hee gives her more information. Open questions make a conversation more interesting.

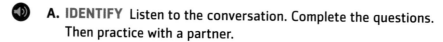

Conversation 1: Closed question	Conversation 2: Open question
A: I visited Hong Kong last week.	A: I visited Hong Kong last week.
B: **Was it fun?**	B: **How was it?**
A: Yes.	A: It was great! I visited a lot of interesting sights, and I tried new food.

A. IDENTIFY Listen to the conversation. Complete the questions. Then practice with a partner.

Emma: John, _____ Greece?

 1

John: Fantastic! I liked Athens a lot. The museums and architecture were great. And the view from the top of the Acropolis was amazing!

Emma: _____?

 2

John: Well, Greeks eat a lot of bread, cheese, olives, and vegetables. For meat, they eat a lot of lamb. I love all of those foods, so I was very happy!

Emma: That sounds great, John.

John: _____ your trip to Mexico City?

 3

Emma: It was good, but I was really busy.

John: That's too bad. _____ Mexico City _____?

 4   5

Emma: Well, it's huge! It's very busy, and the traffic is sometimes awful.

John: Uh-huh. _____ the food?

 6

Emma: It was delicious. We had fresh vegetables and fruit every day.

John: That's great!

the Acropolis in Athens

TIP FOR SUCCESS

Remember to use adverb phrases for time, like *two months ago* and *last year*.

B. CREATE Look at your sentences from Activity C on page 138. Discuss your trip with a partner. Use open questions to find out more information.

A: *I traveled to Moscow, Russia, last year.*
B: *What was it like?*
A: *It was fantastic. Moscow is a beautiful city. I visited . . .*

iQ PRACTICE Go online for more practice with using open questions.
Practice > Unit 7 > Activity 14

Give a presentation about where you want to travel

In this assignment, you are going to give a presentation about a place that you want to visit. Think about the Unit Question, "Where do you want to travel?" Use Listening 1, Listening 2, the unit video, and your work in this unit. Look at the Self-Assessment checklist on page 142.

CONSIDER THE IDEAS

IDENTIFY What does this advertisement show about London? Check (✓) the things below. Then share with a partner.

☐ 1. interesting places to visit

☐ 2. good shopping

☐ 3. natural beauty

☐ 4. great museums

☐ 5. beautiful architecture

☐ 6. historic buildings

☐ 7. culture

☐ 8. a variety of restaurants

☐ 9. clean and safe parks

☐ 10. good public transportation

PREPARE AND SPEAK

A. FIND IDEAS Work in a group of four. Make a list of places that you want to visit. Why do you want to visit each place? Take notes.

B. ORGANIZE IDEAS With your group, look at your notes from Activity A.

- Choose only one place to present to the class. Why do you want to visit this place? Write four reasons.

- Describe what you want to do there.

- If you want, cut out or print photos of the place that you chose. Make an advertisement like the one on page 141.

- Each person chooses a reason to describe and gives information about what you can do there.

- Practice your presentation.

TIP FOR SUCCESS

Give extra information to make your presentation more interesting.

C. SPEAK Take turns presenting information about the place that you chose. Look at the Self-Assessment checklist below before you begin.

iQ PRACTICE Go online for your alternate Unit Assignment.
Practice > Unit 7 > Activity 15

CHECK AND REFLECT

A. CHECK Think about the Unit Assignment as you complete the Self-Assessment checklist.

SELF-ASSESSMENT	Yes	No
My information was clear.	☐	☐
I used vocabulary from this unit.	☐	☐
I used the past tense correctly.	☐	☐
I pronounced past tense verbs with *-ed* correctly.	☐	☐
I asked open questions during our discussions.	☐	☐

B. REFLECT Discuss these questions with a partner or group.

1. What is something new you learned in this unit?

2. Think about the Unit Question—Where do you want to travel? Is your answer different now than when you started this unit? If yes, how is it different? Why?

iQ PRACTICE Go to the online discussion board to discuss these questions.
Practice > Unit 7 > Activity 16

TRACK YOUR SUCCESS

iQ PRACTICE Go online to check the words and phrases you have learned in this unit. *Practice › Unit 7 › Activity 17*

Check (✓) the skills you learned. If you need more work on a skill, refer to the page(s) in parentheses.

NOTE-TAKING	☐ I can take notes in an informal outline. (p. 122)
LISTENING	☐ I can identify frequency words and expressions. (p. 127)
CRITICAL THINKING	☐ I can infer things based on information that I hear. (p. 131)
VOCABULARY	☐ I can use the dictionary to identify word families. (p. 134)
GRAMMAR	☐ I can use the past of *be* and simple past affirmative statements. (pp. 136–137)
PRONUNCIATION	☐ I can pronounce *-ed* endings. (p. 139)
SPEAKING	☐ I can use open questions. (p. 140)

OBJECTIVE ▶ ☐ I can use information and ideas to give a presentation about a place that I want to visit.

Technology

8

NOTE-TAKING	taking notes in a timeline
CRITICAL THINKING	using a timeline
LISTENING	listening for sequence
VOCABULARY	phrases with *get*
GRAMMAR	simple past with regular and irregular verbs
PRONUNCIATION	numbers with *-teen* and *-ty*
SPEAKING	review: using open questions

UNIT QUESTION

How do you use technology?

A. Discuss these questions with your classmates.

1. Look at the photo. What kind of technology do you see?

2. How do you think these people are using the technology?

3. How do you use this type of technology?

B. Listen to *The Q Classroom* online. Match the ideas with the students. Then answer the questions.

1. Yuna _____   a. staying healthy

2. Felix _____   b. social media

3. Sophy _____   c. texting

4. Marcus _____   d. schoolwork

5. Do you use technology in the same ways that the students do?

6. What are some other ways that you use technology?

iQ PRACTICE   Go to the online discussion board to discuss the Unit Question with your classmates. *Practice > Unit 8 > Activity 1*

UNIT OBJECTIVE

Listen to a classroom lecture, a discussion, and a conversation. Use information and ideas to give a presentation about how a classmate uses technology.

A **timeline** is a list of important events and the times that they happened. You can take notes in a timeline to list the events in order. Look at the sample timeline of events in the history of computers.

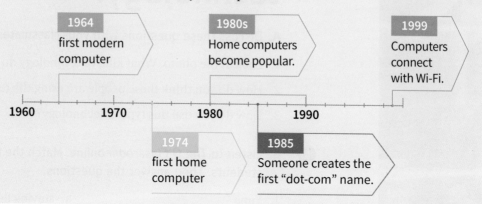

IDENTIFY Listen to a conversation about the history of computer games. Take notes in the timeline as you listen.

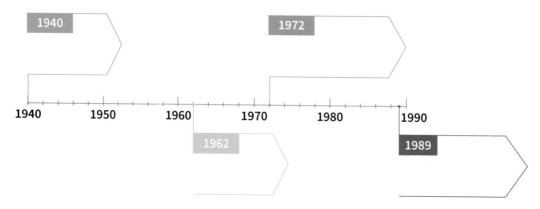

iQ PRACTICE Go online for more practice with taking notes in a timeline. *Practice > Unit 8 > Activity 2*

LISTENING 1

The History of the Cell Phone

You are going to listen to a classroom lecture and discussion about the history of the cell phone. Think about how you use your cell phone.

PREVIEW THE LISTENING

A. VOCABULARY Here are some words and phrases from Listening 1. Read the definitions. Then read the sentences. Which explanation on page 148 is correct? Circle *a* or *b*.

TIP FOR SUCCESS

The phrase *text message* is a noun phrase. When speaking, we usually use the noun *text* instead of the phrase. *Text* can also be a verb. It means "to send a text message."

available *(adjective)* ☌ OPAL ready for you to use, have, or see

information *(noun)* ☌ OPAL facts or details about someone/something

keep in touch *(verb phrase)* to know what is happening with someone/ something

look up *(verb phrase)* to look for information in a dictionary or reference book, or by using a computer

smartphone *(noun)* a cell phone that also has some of the functions of a computer, such as access to the Internet and apps

text message *(noun phrase)* ☌ a written message that you send using your cell phone

work on *(verb phrase)* to try hard to improve or achieve something

☌ Oxford 3000™ words   **OPAL** Oxford Phrasal Academic Lexicon

ACADEMIC LANGUAGE

You can use *available* with or without the preposition *to* after it. You can use different verbs before *available*: **be** available, **become** available, **make** (something) available.

━━━━━━━━━━ OPAL
Oxford Phrasal Academic Lexicon

1. I couldn't go online with my old cell phone. It wasn't a <u>smartphone</u>.

   a. You can go online with a smartphone.

   b. You can't go online with a smartphone.

2. The new cell phone is not <u>available</u> to buyers yet. People can start buying it next Monday.

   a. You can buy the new cell phone now.

   b. You can't buy the new cell phone now.

3. Eric is <u>working on</u> his paper. It's due on Wednesday.

   a. Eric is at work.

   b. Eric is writing his paper.

4. I can send you <u>text messages</u> while I'm at work, but I can't call you.

   a. A text message is the same thing as a phone call.

   b. A text message is not the same thing as a phone call.

5. Margo <u>keeps in touch</u> with her old friends. She likes to know how they're doing.

   a. When you keep in touch with someone, you see or talk to them.

   b. When you keep in touch with someone, you don't see or talk to them.

6. Kay doesn't remember where the computer store is. She has to <u>look</u> it <u>up</u> online.

   a. Kay has to find an address.

   b. Kay wants to buy a computer online.

7. Lee isn't sure which cell phone to buy. She needs some more <u>information</u> about them.

   a. Lee wants to know more about the cell phones.

   b. Lee knows everything about the cell phones.

iQ PRACTICE Go online for more practice with the vocabulary.
Practice > Unit 8 > Activities 3–4

B. PREVIEW You are going to listen to a class lecture and discussion about cell phones. You will hear about some important events in cell phone history and how some people use their cell phones.

1. When do you think cell phones were first available to the public?

2. How do you use your cell phone?

WORK WITH THE LISTENING

A. IDENTIFY Listen to the lecture and discussion. Check (✓) the things that the professor and students talk about.

iQ RESOURCES Go online to download extra vocabulary support.
Resources ▷ Extra Vocabulary ▷ Unit 8

☐ 1. cell phone technology

☐ 2. the meaning of the word *cell*

☐ 3. the first telephone

☐ 4. how many people in the world have cell phones

☐ 5. the first cell phone call

☐ 6. when cell phones were available to buy

☐ 7. how the students use their phones

☐ 8. the best ways to use your cell phone

B. IDENTIFY Listen again. Match the events with the correct years.

1. A mobile phone company starts using the word *cell*. ____   a. 1920s

2. Some people have car phones. ____   b. 1956

3. People start trying to make cell phones. ____   c. 1971

4. Someone makes the first call on a cell phone. ____   d. 1973

5. People send the first text messages. ____   e. 1983

6. The first camera phones are available. ____   f. 1993

7. Cell phones are available to the public. ____   g. 2000

CRITICAL THINKING STRATEGY

Using a timeline

A **timeline** can help you organize and remember the order of important events. When you hear dates, write them down and take notes on the events that happened on those dates. Then create a timeline, and look at the events.

Think about how things changed over time. Think about what things were like *before* the first event on your timeline. Think about what things might be like *after* the last event on your timeline. This helps you understand a topic more deeply.

iQ PRACTICE Go online to watch the Critical Thinking Video and check your comprehension. *Practice ▷ Unit 8 ▷ Activity 5*

C. APPLY Interview a classmate. Using the questions below or your own ideas, find out three important dates relating to his or her experiences with technology. Write the dates and events on the timeline below. Then review the information. What can it tell you about your classmate? Report back to the class.

1. When did you first use a computer? Where did you use it?

2. Do you own a computer or laptop? If so, when did you get your first one?

3. Do you own a smartphone? If so, when did you get your first one?

D. IDENTIFY Complete the timeline with some of the information from Activity B.

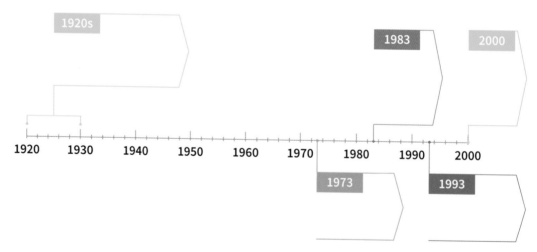

E. IDENTIFY Listen to the lecture and discussion again. Answer the questions.

1. What does the professor ask the students about at the beginning of the class?

    a. the history of cell phones

    b. how they use their cell phones

    c. if they have cell phones

2. According to the professor, what is a *cell*?

    a. an area of a city

    b. a type of smartphone

    c. a part of a phone

3. Who created the first cell phone?

    a. Dr. Martin Cropper

    b. Dr. Marcus Clipper

    c. Dr. Martin Cooper

4. What could people do with the first cell phones?

    a. call people

    b. send texts and call people

    c. send texts, call people, and take photographs

5. How does Padma use her phone?

    a. She plays games and writes emails to her friends and family.

    b. She calls and sends texts to her friends and family.

    c. She calls her friends and sends text messages to her grandparents.

6. How does Franco use his phone?

    a. He writes emails, plays games, and keeps in touch with old friends.

    b. He plays games, shops online, and watches movies.

    c. He looks up information, writes emails, and plays games.

7. How does Ken use his phone?

    a. He shops, listens to books, and plays games.

    b. He listens to music, reads books, and shops.

    c. He reads books, plays games, and looks up information.

 # SAY WHAT YOU THINK

SYNTHESIZE Think about Listening 1, Listening 2, and the unit video as you discuss the questions.

1. How do you feel when you forget your cell phone? Why?

2. Do you think cell phones make life easier or harder? Explain.

3. Imagine that nobody has a cell phone. How is your life different? Think of five examples.

Two or more events happen in a sequence. First one thing happens. Then another thing happens. These words and expressions can help you listen for sequence.

> I had a terrible day.
> **First,** I lost my cell phone.
> **Then** I was late for class.
> **When** I was at school, I dropped my laptop on the ground.
> **Finally,** I failed my math test.

A. IDENTIFY Listen to the conversation. Number the events in the correct order (1–5).

_____ Uncle Jay got his own computer. The screen was blue with yellow words.

_____ Uncle Jay got his first laptop.

__1__ Uncle Jay used computers at school.

_____ Uncle Jay got his tenth computer.

_____ Uncle Jay got a computer when he was 18.

Uncle Jay

B. IDENTIFY Listen to parts of the conversation again. Circle the words and expressions you hear. Some items have more than one answer.

1. first	then	in 1986
2. then	when I was 18	finally
3. first	then	when I was 22
4. in 2019	when I was working	finally

iQ PRACTICE Go online for more practice with listening for sequence.
Practice > Unit 8 > Activity 6

I Can't Get Online!

OBJECTIVE ▶ You are going to listen to a conversation between roommates. Think about how you use the Internet.

PREVIEW THE LISTENING

A. VOCABULARY Here are some words and phrases from Listening 2. Read the definitions. Then complete the sentences below.

> **busy** *(adjective)* 𝕻 working or not free
>
> **happen** *(verb)* 𝕻 OPAL to take place, usually without being planned first
>
> **have trouble with** *(verb phrase)* have problems with
>
> **just** *(adverb)* 𝕻 only
>
> **presentation** *(noun)* 𝕻 OPAL the act of showing or explaining something to others; a meeting in which this happens
>
> **shut down** *(verb phrase)* to make something close or stop working
>
> **type** *(verb)* 𝕻 OPAL to write something using a machine that has keys, such as a computer or a cell phone
>
> **use up** *(verb phrase)* 𝕻 to use something until you have no more

𝕻 Oxford 3000™ words   **OPAL** Oxford Phrasal Academic Lexicon

1. I have to do a _____ on the history of computers for my class. I want to include photos in my talk.

2. James is _____ today. He has to study, go to class, work, and then go to a friend's house.

3. Fidel can _____ so quickly. He can write a long text message in a few seconds.

May looks sad.

4. I always _____ my computer at night. I don't like to leave it on all the time.

5. Did something bad _____ to May? She looks sad.

6. I _____ my tablet nearly every day. It just stops working for no reason.

7. Did you _____ all the paper? I want to print something, but I can't find any paper.

8. I don't need a new laptop. I _____ need a new charger for my old laptop.

iQ PRACTICE Go online for more practice with the vocabulary.
Practice > Unit 8 > Activities 7–8

B. PREVIEW You are going to listen to two roommates talk about a problem with Wi-Fi. Before listening, discuss these questions with a partner.

1. What do you use Wi-Fi for?

2. What do you do when you have problems with Wi-Fi?

WORK WITH THE LISTENING

A. IDENTIFY Read the questions. Listen to the conversation. Then circle the correct answer.

iQ RESOURCES Go online to download extra vocabulary support.
Resources > Extra Vocabulary > Unit 8

1. Where are the people?

   a. at home

   b. at school

   c. at work

2. What is Ali doing?

   a. watching a video

   b. working on his laptop

   c. waiting on the phone

3. When did the Wi-Fi stop working?

   a. this morning

   b. yesterday

   c. this evening

B. CATEGORIZE Read the sentences. Then listen again. Write *T* (true) or *F* (false). Then correct the false statements.

____ 1. When Carlo gets home, he is quiet because Ali is on the phone.

____ 2. There was a problem with the Wi-Fi last week.

____ 3. Carlo has to work on a presentation and watch a video.

____ 4. Ali used the Wi-Fi today.

____ 5. Ali didn't have the Wi-Fi password.

C. IDENTIFY Listen to part of the conversation again. What did Ali do? Number the events in the correct order (1–6).

____ He went to class.

____ He came home and tried to go online.

____ He sent emails.

____ He wrote a paper for English.

____ He did research for his history class.

____ He played video games.

D. IDENTIFY Match the sentence halves to make true statements. Then compare answers with a partner. If necessary, listen again and check your answers.

1. First, Ali ____   a. called tech support.

2. Next, he ____   b. typed in his username and password again.

3. Then he ____   c. unplugged the modem and plugged it back in.

4. Finally, he ____   d. shut down his laptop and started it again.

E. DISCUSS Discuss the questions in a group.

1. What are some things that you can't do when your Wi-Fi stops working?

2. When you can't get online, does that affect your life a lot? Explain.

iQ PRACTICE Go online for additional listening and comprehension.
Practice > Unit 8 > Activity 9

WORK WITH THE VIDEO

VIDEO VOCABULARY

diary (n.) a place where you write what you have done each day

strategy (n.) a plan or a way to achieve something

recommendation (n.) a suggestion or a piece of advice about what to do

A. PREVIEW How many different social media accounts do you have? Do you have trouble following all of them? Why or why not?

iQ RESOURCES Go online to watch the video about a new social media app. *Resources > Video > Unit 8 > Unit Video*

B. IDENTIFY Watch the video two or three times. Then circle the correct answer.

1. There are over (one million / one billion) people on social media sites.

2. People spend (one quarter / one half) of their online time on social media.

3. Esplorio shows (the place you traveled to / all your social media photos).

4. Tim started Esplorio because he realized that all his (friends / travel photos) were on different sites.

5. Isis Innovation gave Tim and Issa (jobs / a place to work).

6. Isis Innovation also helped Tim and Issa create a business (strategy / website).

7. In the future, Esplorio will make (social media / travel) recommendations.

C. EXTEND Do you think a lot of people will use Esplorio? Do you think you will use it? Explain.

SAY WHAT YOU THINK

SYNTHESIZE Imagine that there is no Internet connection for 100 miles around your home. Think about Listening 1, Listening 2, and the unit video as you discuss the questions.

1. How would you spend your time? What would you do?

2. How would your life be different?

BUILDING VOCABULARY Phrases with *get*

There are many phrases with the word *get*. In these phrases, *get* often means *receive* or *become*. The past tense form of *get* is *got*.

Can you get online? Anna got a good price on a new computer.

Here are some more phrases with *get*.

get a good grade	get hired	get married
get an email	get hurt/injured	get out
get angry	get in touch (with)	get together
get better/worse	get lost	get up

Ahmed and Feride

A. APPLY Complete the sentences. Use a phrase with *get* in the simple past.

1. I _____ on my way to your house because my GPS wasn't working.

2. I _____ because a coworker told our boss that I was a bad employee.

3. Ahmed and Feride _____ last weekend. The wedding was really fun.

4. Luke and I _____ this afternoon. We went to a movie.

5. An old friend _____ with me yesterday. It was nice to hear from her.

6. Nina _____ at a great tech company. She's excited about working there.

7. I feel terrible. My cold _____ over the weekend.

8. Tamara _____ on her exam. She studied really hard for it.

9. Lana _____ from Jorge yesterday. He wrote a lot. He's doing great, and he really likes Madrid.

10. Dennis _____ at work this morning. He cut his hand.

B. CREATE Write answers to the questions. Then discuss with a partner.

1. When do you get angry?

2. What do you do when you get lost?

3. How do you feel when old friends get in touch with you?

4. When you want a certain job, what do you do to make sure you get hired?

iQ PRACTICE Go online for more practice with using phrases with *get*.
Practice > Unit 8 > Activity 10

SPEAKING

OBJECTIVE ▶ At the end of this unit, you are going to give a presentation about how a classmate uses technology.

GRAMMAR Simple past with regular and irregular verbs

The simple past describes completed actions in the past.

⌐ The Wi-Fi **stopped** working.   I **called** tech support.

Many verbs have irregular past forms. They don't end in *-ed*.

Irregular past forms

begin	**began**	keep	**kept**	send	**sent**
buy	**bought**	put	**put**	shut	**shut**
get	**got**	read	**read**	think	**thought**
have	**had**	see	**saw**	write	**wrote**

Affirmative statements

subject	verb	
I / You / We / They	**sent**	John a text.
He / She / It	**got**	worse.

Negative statements

subject	*did + not*	verb
I / You / We / They	**did not**	**buy** a new phone.
He / She / It	**didn't**	**arrive** on time.

Yes / *No* questions				Answers	
did	subject	verb		*yes*	*no*
Did	you	**post**	a video?	Yes, I **did**.	No, I **didn't**.
	he	**take**	pictures?	Yes, he **did**.	No, he **didn't**.

Information questions					Answers
wh- word	*did*	subject	verb		past verb
Where		you	**go**	yesterday?	I **went** to my aunt's house.
When	did	he	**call**	you?	He **called** me this morning.
What		they	**buy**?		They **bought** a new laptop.

iQ RESOURCES Go online to watch the Grammar Skill Video.
Resources › Video › Unit 8 › Grammar Skill Video

A. APPLY Complete each sentence. Use the correct simple past form. Some sentences are negative.

1. Ling _____ (buy) a new tablet computer last week.

2. My mother _____ (not / have) a computer until 2015.

3. We _____ (see) a great movie last night.

4. Lisa _____ (have) trouble with her laptop this morning.

5. I _____ (send) you an email yesterday.

6. Amal _____ (write) three papers last week.

7. Ellen _____ (not / call) tech support. She fixed the computer.

8. Leo _____ (not / graduate) last year.

9. Robert _____ (not / give) me his email address.

10. Kate _____ (shut) down her computer and then went to class.

Lisa's laptop isn't working.

B. COMPOSE Look at the underlined information in the answers below. What does the information answer—*when, what, where,* or *why*? Write a question for each answer.

1. Question: _____

   Answer: Emma called me <u>yesterday</u>.

2. Question: _____

   Answer: He got lost <u>because his GPS wasn't working</u>.

3. Question: _____

   Answer: He bought his phone <u>at the mall</u>.

4. Question: _____

   Answer: He got <u>a new tablet computer</u> for his birthday.

Emma called me yesterday.

C. CREATE What did you do yesterday? What *didn't* you do? Write four sentences. Use verbs from the box. Then read your sentences to a partner.

buy	do	give	have	read	study
come	eat	go	play	see	watch

iQ PRACTICE Go online for more practice with the simple past.
Practice > Unit 8 > Activities 11–12

Numbers ending in *-teen* (*13* and *14*) and *-ty* (*30* and *40*) can be difficult to pronounce. These numbers sound similar, but you pronounce the last syllable differently.

Numbers with *-teen* The last syllable starts with a hard *t* sound and ends with *n*.	Numbers with *-ty* The last syllable uses a soft *d* sound, like *dee*.
15 fif-teen	50 fif-ty
16 six-teen	60 six-ty
17 seven-teen	70 seven-ty

A. IDENTIFY Listen to the sentences. Circle the number that you hear. Then practice the sentences with a partner.

1. My cousin is (13 / 30) years old.

2. I got (14 / 40) emails over the weekend.

3. My tablet was (819 / 890) dollars.

4. He called at (6:15 / 6:50).

5. The video is (16 / 60) minutes long.

6. There are (18 / 80) people in my class.

7. His great-grandfather was born in (1914 / 1940).

8. I paid (17 / 70) dollars for my train ticket.

I bought a train ticket.

B. CREATE For each item, write a sentence with one of the numbers. Then read your sentences to a partner. Listen to your partner's sentences. What number do you hear?

1. (13 / 30) _____

2. (14 / 40) _____

3. (15 / 50) _____

4. (16 / 60) _____

5. (17 / 70) _____

iQ PRACTICE Go online for more practice with numbers with *-teen* and *-ty*. *Practice > Unit 8 > Activity 13*

UNIT ASSIGNMENT Interview a classmate and give a presentation

OBJECTIVE ▶ In this assignment, you are going to interview a classmate and give a presentation. Think about the Unit Question, "How do you use technology?" Use Listening 1, Listening 2, the unit video, and your work in this unit. Refer to the Self-Assessment checklist on page 162.

CONSIDER THE IDEAS

CREATE Look at the photos. List the things that you can do with each type of technology.

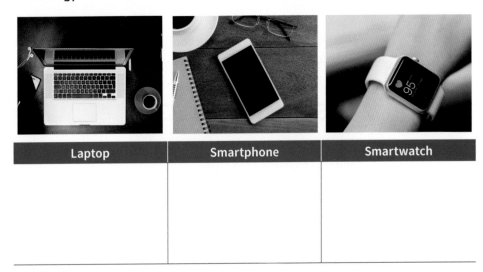

Laptop	Smartphone	Smartwatch

SKILL REVIEW Using open questions

Remember: Ask open questions to get answers with more information. Review the Speaking Skill box in Unit 7 on page 140.

A: I take photos with my phone.
B: **Where do you take photos?**

A: I took an online class.
B: **What class did you take?**

PREPARE AND SPEAK

A. FIND IDEAS Interview a partner. Follow these steps.

1. Start with a general question, like *What types of technology do you use every day?*

2. Ask follow-up questions for details and reasons, for example, *When did you use it last? What did you use it for? Why did you use (your phone) and not (your laptop) for that?*

3. Get information about at least six different ways that your partner uses technology.

B. ORGANIZE IDEAS Choose four of your partner's answers to present to your class.

- Make an outline for your presentation.

- Include at least two details about each way that your partner uses technology.

C. SPEAK Practice your presentation. Then give your presentation to the class (or to a group). Refer to the Self-Assessment checklist below before you begin.

iQ PRACTICE Go online for your alternate Unit Assignment.
Practice > Unit 8 > Activity 14

CHECK AND REFLECT

CHECK Think about the Unit Assignment as you complete the Self-Assessment checklist.

SELF-ASSESSMENT	Yes	No
I was able to speak easily about the topic.	☐	☐
I marked the important information in my notes.	☐	☐
My partner and class understood me.	☐	☐
I used vocabulary from this unit.	☐	☐
I used the past tense correctly.	☐	☐
I used phrases with *get* correctly.	☐	☐
I pronounced numbers correctly.	☐	☐

D. REFLECT Discuss these questions with a partner or group.

1. What is something new you learned in this unit?

2. Look back at the Unit Question—How do you use technology? Is your answer different now than when you started this unit? If yes, how is it different? Why?

iQ PRACTICE Go to the online discussion board to discuss these questions.
Practice > Unit 8 > Activity 15

TRACK YOUR SUCCESS

iQ PRACTICE Go online to check the words and phrases you have learned in this unit. *Practice > Unit 8 > Activity 16*

Check (✓) the skills you learned. If you need more work on a skill, refer to the page(s) in parentheses.

NOTE-TAKING	☐ I can take notes in a timeline. (p. 146)
CRITICAL THINKING	☐ I can use a timeline to organize important events. (p. 149)
LISTENING	☐ I can listen for sequence. (p. 152)
VOCABULARY	☐ I can recognize and use phrases with *get*. (p. 157)
GRAMMAR	☐ I can recognize and use the simple past with regular and irregular verbs. (p. 158)
PRONUNCIATION	☐ I can pronounce numbers with *-teen* and *-ty*. (p. 160)
SPEAKING	☐ I can use open questions. (p. 161)
OBJECTIVE ▶	☐ I can use information and ideas to give a presentation about how a classmate uses technology.

VOCABULARY LIST AND CEFR CORRELATION

🔑 The **Oxford 3000**™ is a list of the 3,000 core words that every learner of English needs to know. The words have been chosen based on their frequency in the Oxford English Corpus and relevance to learners of English. Every word is aligned to the CEFR, guiding learners on the words they should know at the A1–B2 level.

OPAL The **Oxford Phrasal Academic Lexicon** is an essential guide to the most important words and phrases to know for academic English. The word lists are based on the Oxford Corpus of Academic English and the British Academic Spoken English corpus.

The **Common European Framework of Reference for Language (CEFR)** provides a basic description of what language learners have to do to use language effectively. The system contains 6 reference levels: A1, A2, B1, B2, C1, C2.

UNIT 1

belong to *(v. phr.)* 🔑 A2
club *(n.)* 🔑 A1
collect *(v.)* 🔑 A2
good at *(phr.)* 🔑 A1
hobbies *(n.)* 🔑 A1
interested in *(phr.)* 🔑 OPAL A1
team *(n.)* 🔑 A1

UNIT 2

campus *(n.)* 🔑 B1
community *(n.)* 🔑 OPAL A2
download *(v.)* 🔑 A2
foreign language *(n. phr.)* 🔑 A2
online *(adj., adv.)* 🔑 OPAL A1
professor *(n.)* 🔑 A2
skill *(n.)* 🔑 OPAL A1
special *(adj.)* 🔑 A1

UNIT 3

avoid *(v.)* 🔑 OPAL A2
flavor *(n.)* 🔑 B2
ingredient *(n.)* 🔑 B1
memory *(n.)* 🔑 A2
nutritious *(adj.)*
organic *(adj.)* B2
vegetarian *(n.)*

UNIT 4

crowded *(adj.)* 🔑 A2
modern *(adj.)* 🔑 OPAL A1
nature *(n.)* 🔑 OPAL A2
outdoors *(n.)* 🔑 B1
provide *(v.)* 🔑 OPAL A2
relaxing *(adj.)* 🔑 B1
scene *(n.)* 🔑 A2
tradition *(n.)* 🔑 A2

UNIT 5

affordable *(adj.)* B2
comfortable *(adj.)* 🔑 A2
condition *(n.)* 🔑 OPAL A2
demand *(n.)* 🔑 OPAL B2
entertainment *(n.)* 🔑 B1
housing *(n.)* 🔑 B2
increase *(v.)* 🔑 OPAL A2
landlord *(n.)* C1
location *(n.)* 🔑 OPAL B1
noisy *(adj.)* 🔑 A2
private *(adj.)* 🔑 OPAL B1
problem *(n.)* 🔑 OPAL A1
public transportation *(n. phr.)* A2
rent *(n.)* 🔑 B1
roommate *(n.)*
shortage *(n.)* B2

UNIT 6

control *(n.)* 🔑 OPAL A2
depends on *(v. phr.)* 🔑 OPAL A2
diet *(n.)* 🔑 A1
energy *(n.)* 🔑 OPAL A2
exercise *(v.)* 🔑 OPAL A1
healthy *(adj.)* 🔑 A1
lonely *(adj.)* 🔑 B1
manage *(v.)* 🔑 A2
pill *(n.)* B2
produce *(v.)* 🔑 OPAL A2
reduce *(v.)* 🔑 OPAL A2
run-down *(adj.)*
stress *(n.)* 🔑 OPAL A2
vitamin *(n.)* 🔑 B2

UNIT 7

advantage *(n.)* 🔑 OPAL A2
average *(adj.)* 🔑 OPAL A2
climate *(n.)* 🔑 OPAL A2
culture *(n.)* 🔑 OPAL A1
decision *(n.)* 🔑 OPAL A2
disappointed *(adj.)* 🔑 B1
either *(adv.)* 🔑 A2
else *(adv.)* 🔑 A1
experience *(n.)* 🔑 OPAL A2
historic *(adj.)* 🔑 B1
lecture *(n.)* 🔑 OPAL A2
nervous *(adj.)* 🔑 A2
recently *(adv.)* 🔑 OPAL A2
skyscraper *(n.)*
whatever *(pro.)* 🔑 OPAL B1

UNIT 8

available *(adj.)* 🔑 OPAL A2
busy *(adj.)* 🔑 A1
happen *(v.)* 🔑 OPAL A1
have trouble with *(v. phr.)*
information *(n.)* 🔑 OPAL A1
just *(adv.)* 🔑 A1
keep in touch *(v. phr.)*
look up *(v. phr.)*
presentation *(n.)* 🔑 OPAL B1
shut down *(v. phr.)*
smartphone *(n.)*
text message *(n. phr.)* 🔑 A1
type *(v.)* 🔑 OPAL B1
use up *(v. phr.)* 🔑 A1
work on *(v. phr.)* A1

AUTHORS AND CONSULTANTS

AUTHORS

Kevin McClure holds an M.A. in Applied Linguistics from the University of South Florida and has taught English in the United States, China, France, and Japan. In addition to his extensive teaching experience, he has managed language programs and editorial teams working on online courseware. He is now the AI and Assessment Lead for DynEd International in San José, California. He is currently developing and refining intelligent assessments.

Mari Vargo holds an M.A. in English from San Francisco State University. She has taught numerous ESL courses at the university level. She has also written textbooks and online course materials for a wide range of programs, including community colleges, universities, corporations, and primary and secondary schools.

SERIES CONSULTANTS

Lawrence J. Zwier holds an M.A. in TESL from the University of Minnesota. He is currently the Associate Director for Curriculum Development at the English Language Center at Michigan State University in East Lansing. He has taught ESL/EFL in the United States, Saudi Arabia, Malaysia, Japan, and Singapore.

Marguerite Ann Snow holds a Ph.D. in Applied Linguistics from UCLA. She teaches in the TESOL M.A. program in the Charter College of Education at California State University, Los Angeles. She was a Fulbright scholar in Hong Kong and Cyprus. In 2006, she received the President's Distinguished Professor award at CSULA. She has trained ESL teachers in the United States and EFL teachers in more than 25 countries. She is the author/editor of numerous publications in the areas of content-based instruction, English for academic purposes, and standards for English teaching and learning. She is a co-editor of *Teaching English as a Second or Foreign Language* (4th ed.).

CRITICAL THINKING CONSULTANT James Dunn is a Junior Associate Professor at Tokai University and the Coordinator of the JALT Critical Thinking Special Interest Group. His research interests include critical thinking skills' impact on student brain function during English learning as measured by EEG. His educational goals are to help students understand that they are capable of more than they might think and to expand their cultural competence with critical thinking and higher-order thinking skills.

ASSESSMENT CONSULTANT Elaine Boyd has worked in assessment for over 30 years for international testing organizations. She has designed and delivered courses in assessment literacy and is also the author of several EL exam coursebooks for leading publishers. She is an Associate Tutor (M.A. TESOL/Linguistics) at University College, London. Her research interests are classroom assessment, issues in managing feedback, and intercultural competences.

VOCABULARY CONSULTANT Cheryl Boyd Zimmerman is Professor Emeritus at California State University, Fullerton. She specialized in second-language vocabulary acquisition, an area in which she is widely published. She taught graduate courses on second-language acquisition, culture, vocabulary, and the fundamentals of TESOL, and has been a frequent invited speaker on topics related to vocabulary teaching and learning. She is the author of *Word Knowledge: A Vocabulary Teacher's Handbook* and Series Director of *Inside Reading, Inside Writing*, and *Inside Listening and Speaking*, published by Oxford University Press.

ONLINE INTEGRATION Chantal Hemmi holds an Ed.D. TEFL and is a Japan-based teacher trainer and curriculum designer. Since leaving her position as Academic Director of the British Council in Tokyo, she has been teaching at the Center for Language Education and Research at Sophia University in an EAP/CLIL program offered for undergraduates. She delivers lectures and teacher trainings throughout Japan, Indonesia, and Malaysia.

COMMUNICATIVE GRAMMAR CONSULTANT Nancy Schoenfeld holds an M.A. in TESOL from Biola University in La Mirada, California, and has been an English language instructor since 2000. She has taught ESL in California and Hawaii, and EFL in Thailand and Kuwait. She has also trained teachers in the United States and Indonesia. Her interests include teaching vocabulary, extensive reading, and student motivation. She is currently an English Language Instructor at Kuwait University.